WITNESS TO FORGERY

WITNESS TO FORGERY

Memoir of a
Forensic Document Examiner

by
Donald B. Doud

Orchard Knoll Publishers
Elm Grove, Wisconsin

ISBN 978-1-456-30260-3

Printed in the United States of America

Orchard Knoll Publishers

825 Lone Tree Rd

Elm Grove, Wisconsin 53122

Phone: 262-271-1799

Donald B. Doud died in 2005.
Had he lived to see the publication of this manuscript,
Don would surely have dedicated it

to his beloved wife of over half a century,
Jane Foster Doud;

to his children and their families:
John, Catherine, David, and Emily Doud;
Bill, Nancy, Will, Andrew, and Caroline Quinn;,
Bob, Corinne, James, and Kassie Doud.

and to his professional colleagues in
The American Society
of Questioned Document Examiners.

The Doud family extends appreciation and gratitude
to Don's colleagues, friends, and family members
who have helped bring this book to publication.
It was truly a labor of love for all involved.

We especially thank

Ellyn Steinke, Don's long time secretary,
who typed and reviewed the first draft;

Jack Harris, professional colleague and friend,
who offered encouragement and valuable advice
throughout the writing of the manuscript;

Lois Ralph, relative and friend, for her patient review,
careful formatting, and help with final details;

Richard S. Wheeler, author and relative,
for his editing expertise and invaluable literary wisdom.

Contents

CONTENTS

Foreword

Donald Budlong Doud was born June 1, 1916, in Wisconsin, but lived most of his early life in California. Mr. Doud, who had a background in photography, began his training in questioned document examination during World War II when he was hired by Clark Sellers to assist in trial preparation. He also took classes in questioned document examination taught by John L. Harris at the University of Southern California. After working for Mr. Sellers for six years, he worked for more than a year in the office of Albert D. Osborn in New York, followed by a year with Herbert J. Walter in Chicago. In 1951, he settled in Milwaukee with John F. Tyrell. Mr. Tyrell passed away in 1955 and Mr. Doud continued to work in private practice in Milwaukee for many years.

Donald Doud was the eighth president of the American Society of Questioned Document Examiners. In addition to the presidency of the Society, Mr. Doud served as Chairman of the Questioned Documents Section of the American Academy of Forensic Sciences and on the board of the American Board of Forensic Document Examiners. He lectured for twenty years before Fred

Inbau's scientific evidence classes at Northwestern University, as well as the Ford Foundation Prosecutor's and Defense Attorneys annual seminars. He was the author of numerous published articles and professional papers. He wrote the monograph "Scientific Evidence" for the 1959 Wisconsin Lawyers' Seminars.

Donald Doud was awarded the 2005 Albert S. Osborn Award of Excellence, presented by the American Society of Questioned Document Examiners.

John J Harris, Past President
American Society of Questioned Document Examiners

A Family Tribute

In his obituary, we children (Robert, Nancy, and John) wrote a few brief words to describe who this remarkable man was to those who loved and cherished him.

> Don loved photography, the north woods, and was an avid fisherman. He was committed to his Congregational church, to his Milwaukee Rotary Club, and to his career as an Examiner of Questioned Documents. Don was a true wordsmith, and was known for his sense of humor and his remarkable Christmas letters. Above all, Don loved his family and inspired them through his positive example of generosity, integrity, and open communication.

Dad used to say to us it was a miracle that he outlived the doctors who had informed him in his teens that he wouldn't live past the age of forty because of multiple health problems. Well into his 80s, Dad would say to us that he couldn't believe how he had made it so long and that he was able to enjoy such a fulfilling life, and experience such interesting times with so many good people. He was amazed that his life was filled with these wonderful and beautiful events: marriage to his beloved wife Jane, three creative and independent children, a fascinating career (detailed in this book), and an exciting and rewarding life of joy surrounded by devoted friends and family.

Dad's life was one of integrity; he believed in it, talked about it, and lived it. Regarding his work as a document examiner, his colleagues remarked that Don could spot a fake because he was so genuine himself. He was a self made man with a reputation for honesty and scientific diligence. Dad explained to us, "Whether it's a document or a human being, call it as you see it. Don't let anyone else tell you how or what to think—do your own research and think for yourselves. Be kind...be fair...be humble, and remember that we stand on each other's shoulders." He was so unassuming and modest, though we all knew he was famous. Dad taught us to ask good questions, to be inclusive and inquisitive, truthful, and loving. He taught us to live in the arena of life rather than on the apathetic sidelines, to never shy away from conflict or controversy in politics or religion, in our careers, and with our friends and family.

Donald Doud: His life and memory is for us a great blessing.

John Doud
Nancy Quinn
Robert Doud

Preface

I belong to one of the smallest and least understood professions in the world. I am a questioned document examiner—better known today as a "forensic document examiner," and I've been working in this mysterious and fascinating field for fifty years.

My cases have been big and small. I've exposed petty forgers and uncovered fake wills, literary frauds, and back-dated records. Some of my cases, such as the 1972 Chicago election frauds, the infamous Alger Hiss espionage-by-typewriter case, and the Clifford Irving-Howard Hughes autobiography hoax, have made front-page headlines all over the world and have shaped history.

As a young man, I was taught my craft by three of the great pioneers in the field, men made famous when they testified in the Lindbergh kidnaping trial.

This memoir is the story of my half-century career as a scientific examiner of documents and as a courtroom warrior. It is the story of truth and science versus fraud and deception, a tale laden with drama, conflict, and controversy, where good does not always triumph over evil.

Take a seat in the jury box, listen to the testimony, carefully study the exhibits, then make your decision. You decide whether Alger Hiss was a spy whose typewriter was used to copy confidential government communiques, whether the "Mormon will" was a forgery or genuinely written by Howard Hughes. This is your chance to relive, indeed participate in, some of the most important cases of the twentieth century.

Welcome to the fascinating and little-known world of the forensic document examiner.

1

Where There's a Will
There's a Way:
A Taste of
Texas Six-Shooter Justice

Truth will come to light...in the end truth will out.
WILLIAM SHAKESPEARE, *The Merchant of Venice*

Resplendent in his black robe, Judge Sinfre, District Court judge for Grayson County, Texas, scowled when I stepped into the witness box and identified myself as a questioned document examiner. When I described the Milwaukee and Chicago locations of my laboratories, his eyes rolled upward as though to say, "Good heavens, what could be worse than having a Yankee expert trying to tell us down here in Texas whether someone's handwriting is genuine or forged." Therefore, I was not too surprised when an arm was thrust over the side of the bench during my swearing-in to plant my left hand firmly on the *Bible* and to make sure I had my right hand pointed directly to heaven when I promised "to tell the truth, the whole truth, and nothing but the truth, so help me God."

This unconventional performance by Judge Sinfre was not lost on attorney Bruce Graham, who had just called me as his first witness for the day. "Don't let him bother you," he whispered. "The jurors are the ones you have to worry about." I swivelled my chair around to face the jury of middle-aged farmers and townsfolk, and smiled into stony faces.

The case that brought me to this musty old courthouse in Sherman, Texas, involved the estate of a wealthy landowner, C. T. Tatum, whose last will and testament, drafted by his own lawyers in 1945, left the bulk of his holdings to the Scottish Rite Hospital for Crippled Children and Buchner Orphans Home, both of Dallas, Texas. The probate of this will was moving along smoothly when, out of the blue came a second will, this time handwritten, leaving everything to Nettie Edna Womble, the old man's housekeeper of nineteen years. The crippled children and orphans would get nothing.

Dubbed by the press as the "Womble will," the document was supposedly written by Tatum on December 9, 1952, and then turned over to Womble for safekeeping—at least that's what she claimed at the probate hearing. The old man died on December 19, 1952, ten days after the date on the questioned document. I was on the stand as an expert witness, prepared to testify that the will was a forgery, an attempted imitation of Tatum's genuine handwriting.

2

WHERE THERE'S A WILL THERE'S A WAY

Bruce Graham, attorney for the orphans and crippled children, had started to question me about my education, experience, and training, a legal requirement for qualifying me as an expert witness, when Womble's junior attorney burst into the courtroom and marched down the aisle with a pair of well dressed, middle-aged gentlemen following closely behind. The judge halted my testimony while the two newcomers were seated at the counsel table with Womble's senior attorneys, one of whom broke the silence with a startling statement: "Your Honor, these two gentlemen are questioned document examiners employed by the United States government in Washington, D. C. They are here at our request and are prepared to testify that the handwritten will produced by Miss Womble is genuine!"

From my vantage point on the witness stand, I almost blurted out, "How in hell could they possibly reach that opinion?" But I had learned to expect surprises in this no-holds-barred lawsuit between Nettie Edna Womble and the orphans and crippled children named in Tatum's original will. Starting with my initial examination of the handwriting evidence in the Collin County courthouse at McKinney, Texas, to the second jury verdict a year and a half later in Sherman, Texas, this case was packed with surprises. Some of them I would just as soon forget.

It all started in 1954 when I was called down to McKinney to examine what was described by Dallas attorney Bruce Graham as a "mysterious" holographic will supposedly written by wealthy landowner C. T. Tatum. My companion on the ride from the airport in Houston to McKinney was George Lacy, friend and fellow document examiner, who had recommended me as a second expert in the case. Lacy, an intense, six-foot man in his mid-fifties, was a Texan from the top of his ten-gallon hat to the soles of his cowboy boots. In court, cross-examining attorneys who questioned the objectivity and accuracy of his findings could expect a reproving, sometimes angry, lecture from Lacy on the propriety of misrepresenting his role as an unbiased scientific witness.

Like a chameleon, Lacy became an entirely different person when he donned his white laboratory coat for an examination of documents in his Houston laboratory. Using the latest in scientific equipment, some of which he designed himself, Lacy conducted careful, objective examinations of disputed documents. Woe to the lawyer who assumed that employing George Lacy would automatically entitle him to a favorable opinion. Lacy once threw a client out of his office for such a suggestion.

Driving close to ninety miles per hour along Route 75 from Houston to McKinney, while I desperately hung onto the edges of my seat to keep from flying through the air, Lacy explained some of the history behind the "Womble will" case.

C. T. Tatum had been an astute businessman who had made lots of money, in land deals and farming, in and around Collin County. Never married, Tatum developed an interest in children's causes and during his lifetime gave substantial amounts of money to the Scottish Rite Hospital for Crippled Children and the Buckner Orphan Home, both of Dallas, Texas. In 1945 when he became ill,

4

he drafted a will that would take care of the children after his death. Among several smaller bequests was one to Nettie Edna Womble, his longtime housekeeper. She was awarded $10,000 in cash, 150 acres of farmland, an automobile, and various household articles.

After Tatum died in 1952, Womble told executors for the Tatum estate how pleased she was to be rewarded so handsomely for merely doing a good job for her employer. But a few weeks later, Womble's mood changed when the estate foolishly refused her demand for more money to pay the inheritance tax liability.

Unaware of Womble's discontent, the Tatum estate executors started procedures for distributing his wealth according to terms of the 1945 will. But they hadn't contended with Nettie Edna Womble, who marched into court announcing that not only had she been Tatum's housekeeper but his lover as well. Although never officially married, they had lived together as husband and wife. She was, in fact, his common-law widow. The reason she hadn't mentioned it before was the private nature of the relationship. When she finally told her lawyers about it, they had advised her that Texas laws placed her on shaky grounds legally, but out of the goodness of their hearts, Tatum's executors might give her a somewhat bigger portion of the old man's estate. They were right about that.

Realizing they had made a mistake with the inheritance tax issue and anxious to get rid of a potentially growing problem, executors for the Tatum estate struck an agreement with Womble. She was to get an additional sum of $25,000 plus 473 acres of land.

Womble promptly accepted the deal and signed a release promising no further demands upon the estate.

But the Tatum estate had not seen the last of Nettie Edna Womble. A month after signing the release, she had a new surprise for them. She had found another will, a more current, handwritten will that Tatum had entrusted to her care shortly before his death. The will left Tatum's entire estate to her. She had discovered the document in her quilt box some time ago but had not said anything about it because she didn't think a handwritten will was legal in Texas. Now she knew differently.

Unbelievable as that story might have been, the lure of Tatum's $2,000,000 estate was sufficient to attract financial and legal support for Womble's cause. This, in turn, led to eighteen months of contentious litigation, in which Lacy and I found ourselves at the very center.

Upon arriving in McKinney, Lacy pulled his car up in front of the only available hotel in town—a rundown relic that could easily have been on the set of a John Wayne western. So, perhaps I should not have been too surprised when Lacy, a former Texas Ranger, knocked on the rickety door of our connecting hotel rooms to introduce me to the facts of life about Texas lawsuits, especially those involving large sums of money. Popping open the top of his suitcase, Lacy pulled out two enormous Texas six-shooters and handed one of them to me. "Don," he said, "do you know how to use one of these babies?" Noticing the look of panic on my face, he continued, "Now, I don't want y'all to be alarmed, but I've been through cases of this kind before, and we've gotta be prepared for the worst. There's lots of money involved here, and I wouldn't be surprised if someone tried to run us out of town."

Being run out of town at gunpoint wasn't something I had anticipated. Up in Milwaukee and Chicago, we had aggressive lawyers and stupid, bullying judges, but I had never felt the need to be armed. Responding to my obvious horror, Lacy quickly slipped the six-shooters back in his bag. I hoped I would never see them again, or any others, during my stay in Texas.

The Collin County courthouse in McKinney was typically situated in the middle of the town square. As Lacy and I walked up the long flight of steps leading to the front door, we were met by a court official who quickly ushered us down the hall, past the ever-present news reporters and curiosity seekers, and into the small room where we were to examine the "Womble will." Attorneys for the orphans and crippled children and Nettie Edna Womble had already arrived and were busily engaged in glaring at each other across one end of the long table set up for our examination. As I bent over to place my case of examination equipment on the floor, I glanced at the hips visible beneath the table for any unnatural bulges in the shape of Texas six-shooters. There were none.

Lacy and I conducted entirely independent examinations of the "Womble will" evidence, so I had no idea what his reaction was to the almost childlike scribbling on the highly touted document. Mine was one of restrained suspicion. Under low-power magnification, I could see that the handwriting was wavy, poorly

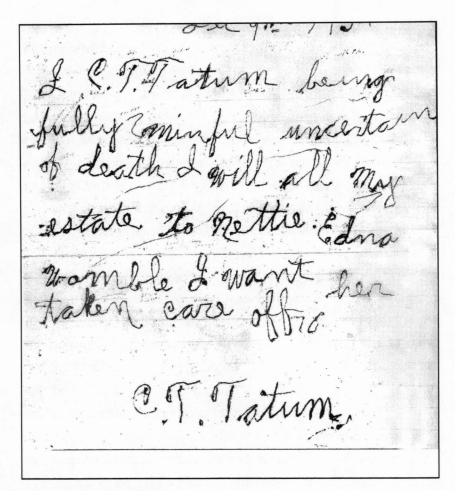

Purported will of C. T. Tatum.

aligned, and overwritten in various parts, typical signs of attempted imitation. But I had also noticed some of those same features in Tatum's known writing, which had deteriorated considerably during the final years of his life. Could Tatum's illness and

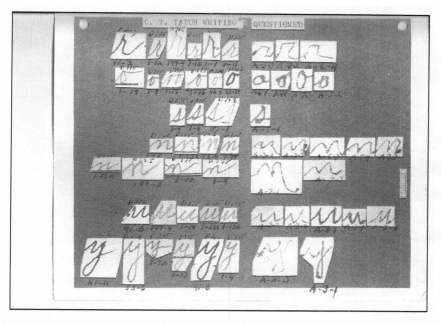

Comparison exhibit showing fundamental differences between Tatum's Spencerian writing habits (left) and the Womble will forgeries (right column).

advanced age have caused the strange, aberrant appearance of the "Womble will" writing?

Then I discovered something in the evidence that jolted me right out of my chair and caused Womble's attorneys to lean across the table to see what I had found. Like remembering the face of a friend you hadn't seen for years, I suddenly recognized in Tatum's genuine writing accents of the Spencerian writing system taught to elementary school children in the United States between 1860 and 1890. Turning to the "Womble will," I looked for evidence of this same style of penmanship and found nothing but a few inept attempts to imitate Tatum's Spencerian capitals and numerals. The writer of the "Womble will" had been taught an entirely different system of writing, and it appeared to be similar to the Palmer method I had learned as a school child in the late 1920s. In terms of their handwriting, the writer of the "Womble will" and Mr. Tatum were of different generations. On this basis alone, not even considering other suspicious features of the handwriting, Tatum could not possibly have written the will.

As I jotted down the results of my examination on a note pad and completed taking photographs with my portable 4 x 5 camera, I could hardly contain my excitement over the weight of evidence I had accumulated—evidence that literally forced me to the conclusion that the "Womble will" was a forgery. I later learned from Bruce Graham that Lacy had reached the same opinion.

The first trial of the "Womble will" contest took place in April of 1955 in the same Collin County courthouse where I had made my initial examination. Tatum had lived most of his life in Collin County, as had members of the jury, the judge, and probably most of the spectators who had come to the courtroom to see the drama unfold.

Both Lacy and I testified at the two-week-long trial, testimony that was largely uneventful except for some heated exchanges between Lacy and the local cross-examining attorney. When my turn came, I expected a similar type of cross-examination, but the judge overruled many of the questions asked me, and those that remained didn't bring forth the answers my interrogator expected. I had the feeling that Womble's lawyers were groping for, but unable to find, a way to cope with the overwhelming evidence of forgery Lacy and I were able to demonstrate by means of our enlarged comparison exhibits.

As I concluded my testimony and stepped down from the witness stand, I felt good about this jury. They had listened attentively to my testimony as well as Mr. Lacy's and seemed particularly impressed by the differences I pointed out in Tatum's Spencerian writing habits. I suspected that everyone else in the courtroom, including the judge, the spectators, and even Womble's own lawyers, were convinced that the will was a forgery. When it came time to present Womble's side of the case, only Nettie Womble herself was able to testify to the genuineness of the will, and even she proved to be a weak and vulnerable witness.

At the conclusion of the trial, the jury deliberated for several days, which was not a good sign. Back in court with their verdict, the foreman announced that they were unable to reach a unanimous verdict. Out of the twelve-member jury panel, there was one holdout who would not budge from his opinion that the "Womble will" was genuine. With Texas law requiring a unanimous verdict in jury cases, the judge, amid rumors of jury tampering and payoffs, was finally forced to declare a mistrial.

So here I was, a year later, at the second trial in Sherman, Texas, again prepared to testify that the "Womble will" was a forgery. I was preceded by George Lacy, who had testified for two long days. The judge helped drag the proceedings out by allowing Womble's attorney to take cheap shots at Lacy during cross-examination. At one point after a particularly heated exchange, Lacy smiled broadly at the cross-examiner as though to say, "Now, even though that was a misleading question, I forgive you for asking it." In exasperation, the opposing lawyer shouted, "Mr. Lacy, you keep smiling all the time; is there something funny about me or this trial?"

To which Lacy responded, "No, sir, I was just trying to be pleasant so the jury wouldn't think I was getting mad at you for those misleading questions." Because the judge failed to control the proceedings, the testimony of Lacy dragged on, to a point where the jury became noticeably irritated and bored.

Being present in the courtroom during Lacy's cross-examination gave me an idea of the kind of cross-examination I might encounter when my turn came to testify. But nothing could have prepared me for the unbelievable event that occurred when I finally took the witness stand—the interruption of my testimony by two government experts prepared to testify that "the 'Womble will' is genuine."

They missed it, I thought to myself. They didn't catch the generational difference between Tatum's writing and the handwriting on the "Womble will." Had they properly studied the evolution of writing systems in the United States, they would have immediately grasped the significance of this evidence.

When Judge Sinfre finally gave his grudging approval for me

to continue my testimony, I set out in earnest to educate the jury on the subject of forgery and handwriting systems. Using a large pad, I showed them how difficult it is for one person to simulate the handwriting habits of another and the inevitable results of such an attempt. I showed them textbook examples of the Spencerian writing system followed by Tatum and how the forger of the

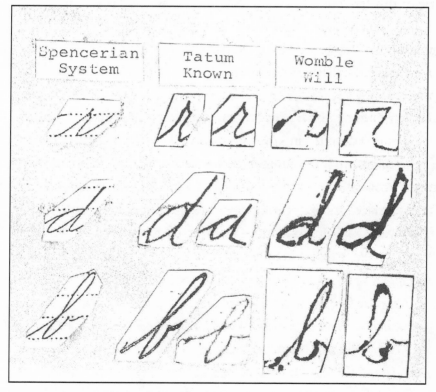

Left: Letters *r*, *d* and *b* from Spencerian textbook. Center: Same letters from C. T. Tatum's known writing. Right: Examples from Womble will. Note flat topped *r*, *d*s with loops and *b*s with shallow bowl formations.

"Womble will" had failed to copy the basic forms. I showed them letter and word comparison exhibits to drive home each point. Repeating the statement I had made at the outset of my testimony, I concluded by saying, "The combination of fundamental differences in writing habits convinces me beyond a reasonable doubt that the 'Womble will' is a forgery. It was neither written, dated, nor signed by C. T. Tatum." Then I turned to the jury for their reaction, but all I saw were inscrutable faces. From the scowl on Judge Sinfre's face, there could be little doubt about his feelings.

On cross-examination, I expected a hammer-and-tong attack by Womble's attorney on my limited experience as a questioned document examiner (I was still fairly new to the profession) or his taking exception to my use of outside information such as what I obtained from the Spencerian Business College in Milwaukee. Instead, he wisely left the Spencerian issue pretty much alone and concentrated, instead, on my statement that certain characters in the "Womble will" differed from Tatum's customary writing habits. For example, I had stated that the closed top to the letter *a* in the will signatures differed from Tatum's customary habits of writing the letter with an open top. To make his point that the *a* wasn't different, Womble's counsel went through 482 checks signed by Mr. Tatum during the latter years of his life and handed me four examples where the *a* was closed or partially closed at the top. When I tried to explain to the jury that a variation of one percent, especially in the handwriting of an older person, was well within the norm of "customary" writing habits, the judge ordered my explanation stricken from the record.

On redirect examination, Bruce Graham attempted to set the record straight by injecting a little humor into the proceedings. "Mr. Doud," he said, "do you know how long it took all six of those lawyers to search through the 492 checks of Mr. Tatum's to find those four little *a* s?"

"No," I answered, "but it looks like they have been working very hard." My testimony concluded shortly thereafter, the attorneys for the orphans and crippled children rested their case.

It was now time for Womble's attorneys to prove that the handwritten will found in the quilt box had been written by Mr. Tatum. Their chief witness, Nettie Womble, stood by her story of when and how she found the will but made no mention of any common-law-wife relationship between herself and Tatum. A more difficult person to cross-examine than at the first trial, she cast herself in the role of a long-suffering servant of the old gentleman who was finally rewarded in the end for her unselfish sacrifices.

The two government men now took the witness stand, one after the other, and were qualified as questioned document examiners. Bruce Graham strenuously fought to keep them from testifying based upon a long-time government rule prohibiting experts employed by federal bureaus from testifying in private cases. But Judge Sinfre dismissed this objection with a wave of his hand and smiled when the two testified that the "Womble will" was genuine—Lacy and I were wrong in saying it was a forgery.

15

I was sitting in the spectator area watching the entire proceedings and was shocked at the lack of professionalism exhibited by both men. Offering opinions with no comparison exhibits of any kind to back them up, they said that the systemic differences I had pointed out were, in fact, "natural variations" in the writing. The clumsy, drawn appearance of the "Womble will" writing, including the mending of strokes where the writer had altered letter shapes after the fact, was due to Tatum's advanced age and poor health. They seemed to be more interested in attacking the evidence of forgery Lacy and I had found than presenting logical reasons for their own opinions. Being familiar with the excellent training programs conducted by the FBI and other government agencies, I wondered about the seeming lack of qualifications of these two men. Therefore, I was not too surprised when, on cross-examination, Bruce Graham brought out the fact that one of the government experts devoted only a fraction of his time to examining documents and the other's job was more administrative than technical. Nevertheless, when I glanced at the jurors to get their reactions to the testimony, they seemed to ignore these facts.

At the conclusion of Womble's case, there followed an afternoon of closing arguments by both sides. These proceedings were unusual, to say the least. To paraphrase a portion of the attacks on my testimony, Womble's attorney stated: "That Mr. Dude or Mr. Doud, or whatever his name is, from way up north in Milwaukee, he comes down here to Texas to try to tell us that Mr.

Tatum's will is a forgery. Don't you believe him." Lacy's testimony was dealt with even more harshly and the government experts lauded for their competency in trying to set the record straight about the "Womble will" and the object of its largess. It was on that note that the Womble will contest ended.

Unlike the lawyers, plaintiffs, and defendants involved in trials, I am never an advocate for one side or the other. I am an objective scientist seeking to find the truth in the documents I examine. But being objective does not mean that I am disinterested in the results of my efforts, especially when the document I examined is at the center of a hotly contested legal controversy.

The "Womble will" contest was one of those cases. I had spent literally hundreds of hours examining documents, reviewing evidence, and testifying in court. The jury in the first trial had reached an almost unanimous verdict that the will was a forgery, and I was exceedingly anxious to learn whether the second jury could reach full agreement. But I was totally unprepared for the telephone call I received from Bruce Graham two days after my return to Milwaukee. "Mr. Doud," he said, "we lost the case! The jury came out with a unanimous verdict against the orphans and crippled children. They found the 'Womble will' to be genuine."

I almost dropped the phone in disbelief. Was there something about my testimony or that of Lacy that antagonized the jury? Were they unduly influenced by the testimony of the two experts from the United States government? Was it the hostile attitude of Judge Sinfre and the acrimony poisoning the atmosphere of the trial?

My friend, professor Jim Fisher, calls verdicts of this kind "jury nullification." For some reason or another, the jurors became sympathetic to Nettie Womble and were persuaded that Tatum wanted to reward her with the entire proceeds from his estate. But in the end, the verdict they reached didn't really matter. The Texas Supreme Court did what the Sherman jury should have done in the first place. They threw out the "Womble will"—not on the grounds that it was forged but because Womble knew of the will's existence in her quilt box at the time she accepted final settlement from the Tatum estate and signed the release. By signing a release, she forfeited any rights under the will.

So in the end, Buckner Orphan Home and the Scottish Rite Hospital for Crippled Children received the bequests set forth in Tatum's 1945 will. Womble received nothing but her original inheritances, a tarnished reputation in Collin County, and some unpaid bills. I received a liberal education in Texas six-shooter justice.

2

Launching a Career — The Hard Way

My Three-Year Battle with TB Had Its Own Rewards

The life-threatening illness I battled for three years during my late teens was not the best way of preparing me for the stress and physical demands of cases like the Tatum will contest of Sherman, Texas. But somehow or other I managed to survive and even achieve a few goals—aided, I must admit, by some miraculous events that happened at exactly the right time and in exactly the right sequence.

The year was 1937. I was nineteen years of age and living with my widowed mother and older brother in a suburb of Los Angeles. Unable to continue my schooling because of constantly recurring colds and influenza, I finally developed a hacking cough and consistently began to lose weight. After a series of x-rays and sputum tests, the doctors solemnly informed me that I had an advanced case of tuberculosis involving lesions on the right lung. In order to have any chance of survival, I must have complete bed rest and treatment, preferably in a hospital setting. Shortly thereafter, an opening appeared at Barlow Sanatorium on Chavez Ravine Road in Los Angeles, and I was transported there posthaste.

I can still remember the feelings of despair and not a little terror than engulfed me as I lay on the small hospital bed at Barlow that I was destined to occupy for the next two years. I have never been more depressed in my life. But then there was a knock on the door, and into the room bounded an energetic little grey-haired lady who introduced herself as Mrs. Heiskel, the sanatorium librarian. "The patients here all call me Mama," she said with a smile, and it didn't take me long to realize why. Noticing the dejected expression on my face, she sat down on the side of my bed and, taking my hand in hers, proceeded to tell me about hospital routine, the medical steps that might be necessary to cure me of TB, and of her beloved library. "Boredom is the worst enemy you will have to face, Mr. Doud," she said, "and I have hundreds of books and magazines on any subject to keep you busy."

True to her word, Mama Heiskel kept me supplied with books throughout my stay at Barlow, many on subjects I chose but others on academic subjects she thought I should study. Knowing of my interest in photography—I had won several photo awards during my high school years—she kept me supplied with books on photography and magazines such as *Popular Photography*. During my later association with Clark Sellers, I wrote an article, with help from my brother Chuck, titled, "Photography Foils the Forger," which to my surprise was accepted and published by that magazine.

Science was my major interest in high school, and on one occasion I remember well, Mama Heiskel plopped down on my bedside table an armful of *Scientific American* magazines and a Sherlock Holmes mystery. I was completely taken by Holmes' remarkable reasoning ability, eye for detail, and his early use of scientific evidence to help him solve crimes. Always with a keen eye out for the future vocations of those of us who managed to survive the medical ordeals of those days, Mama Heiskel narrowed in on both fictional and non-fictional accounts of scientific crime investigations, a subject with which I became more and more enamored. I owe much to Mama Heiskel who had that rare ability to uplift the patients with whom she came in contact and to teach them that adversity and discouragement can be overcome by willpower and absorbing one's self in new learning experiences.

My stay at Barlow was before the time of the miraculous modern medication that destroys tuberculosis bacillus in a matter of weeks or months. Cures in my day, "arrested cases" as they were then called, were measured in years—years of strict bed rest with feet never touching the floor, usually accompanied by collapsed-lung therapy (pneumothorax). In these circumstances, the doctors, nurses, librarian, and other patients surrounding you assume tremendous importance and are at the very center of your life.

The fellow patient I remember best was Clark Jacobs, a skinny, humorous ex-police investigator from the nation's hotspot, El Centro, California. Jacobs was a most interesting and innovative person who liked nothing better than to amuse and shock those of us who were still confined to bed. As an ambulatory patient, Jacobs would come back from his afternoon walks up Chavez Ravine Drive (also known as Lover's Lane) with tantalizing accounts of illicit romance and intrigue. "Guess what I saw today," he would say and tell how he not only spied upon lovers, including one or two of our own off-duty nurses, smooching in parked cars, but also found to his delight that some of them left behind incriminating evidence in the form of letters torn into small pieces and scattered on the ground. He would gather these up in envelopes, "just as we used to do when I was with the El Centro police," he would tell us, and take them back to the infirmary for us to reconstruct. How well I remember painstakingly trying to fit the torn pieces of these documents together, much like jigsaw puzzles, hoping that Jacobs had found enough of the pieces to make an intelligible message. One brief but revealing note said, as nearly as I can recall, "Darling, John is out of town on a business trip. Can we meet at the usual place at 4 PM tomorrow?" In my later career as a questioned document examiner, I examined several cases involving torn letters and used some of the same reconstruction techniques that Jacobs demonstrated during my stay at Barlow.

Knowing of my growing interest in scientific evidence, Jacobs would also visit me in the infirmary to discuss some new murder investigation he had read about in the paper or to chat about past cases he had worked on while he was with the El Centro Police Department. I owe much to Clark Jacobs, for he was not only a good friend, but he also introduced me to some of the glamorous and not-so-glamorous aspects of scientific crime investigations.

After two years of bed rest and another year as an ambulatory patient, I was finally released from Barlow as an "arrested case" and started looking around for work that would fit my almost non-existent qualifications. The life of a police investigator sounded exciting and challenging, but it was also rigorous work demanding long hours and exposure to all types of elements, both weather and criminal. My health history would certainly militate against that occupation.

Photography—now there was a field that offered all sorts of possibilities, and for a brief period I accepted employment as a pay-per-shot sports photographer. My last assignment was to photograph a boxing event involving two evenly matched young fighters. After furiously shooting off a roll of film during the early part of the bout, I was busily engaged in loading new film in the camera when the most unusual of all boxing events took place—a double knockout, no less. This bit of bad timing got me fired and signaled the end of my career as a sports photographer.

Studying with Ansel Adams, Photographic Genius: He Tempted Me to Become a Pictorial Photographer

In the summer of 1941 I attended a one-semester course in photography at the Art Center School in Los Angeles given by Ansel Adams, who had already achieved considerable fame for his photographs of Yosemite and other western sites, and by Fred Archer, portrait instructor. The creativeness and enthusiasm of these two men might well have persuaded me to make photography my life career but for one caveat—the amount of darkroom time required. The beautiful photographs Adams now exhibited around the world depended equally as much on his darkroom work—developing the negatives and making prints—as on his camera. Among my most vivid recollections is watching Adams develop films according to the "zone" method, a unique procedure he and Fred Archer had recently perfected involving the matching of film development to the contrast range of the original scene and exposure time. Using a foul smelling, almost worn-out developer, a film desensitizer, and a dim green light for illumination, Adams would carefully immerse the 8 x 10 negative of a high-contrast scene into the developer and then leave it undisturbed, not for the recommended time of seven minutes but for an hour or more of development. When the time was nearly up, he would then resume agitation and inspection of the film under the green light. Finally, like a gourmet cook preparing a choice soufflé, he would say, "There, it's done" and jerk the film from the developer into the stop bath and finally into the fixer. After the final washing process, he would hold the negative up to a light box for him to critically analyze, and for me to wonder at, the astonishing range of tones obtained by this procedure.

Wallace Stegner, *Ansel Adams Images 1923-1974* (Boston: New York Graphic Society, 1974)

Ansel Adams had a remarkable ability to mentally visualize the final results of his photography before ever pushing the button. A field trip our group took to Griffith Park illustrates the point. While all of his students were scurrying around looking for some spectacular scene to photograph, I saw Adams kneeling on the ground with his 8 x 10 view camera focused on some ordinary-appearing ferns. When I asked Adams if I could look at the upside-down image appearing on

My photo of Griffith Park ferns, titled "Woman in Ferns", taken July 1941.

the ground glass, he said, "Well, of course you may." What I saw was a beautifully organized composition of only three or four fern fronds covered with droplets of morning dew, all sharply focused to reveal the delicate, lace-like beauty of each leaf. I cannot recall specifically how this photograph turned out, but in Wallace Stegner's book, *Ansel Adams Images 1923-1974*, there is a similar photograph of ferns taken at Mount Rainier National Park, Washington, that conveys the same ephemeral quality I viewed on the ground glass of Adams' camera. I returned to this same spot later in the day to make my own fern photographs but, like most amateurs, made the mistake of including too much in the photograph, including a prominent female center of interest. Upon viewing my developed photograph, Adams remarked with a twinkle in his eye that perhaps my talents were more suited to feminine fashion photography.

While I learned much from Ansel Adams and was enthralled by his work, I still could not visualize myself taking photographs for the rest of my life, including spending half of that time in the confining space of a darkroom. My thoughts again returned to scientific crime investigations. There had to be something that would require my photographic talents in a less demanding way.

And the end men looked for cometh not,
And a path is there where no man thought

EURIPEDES

Almost as though he had read my mind, I received a call from Clark Jacobs, my old friend from Barlow Sanatorium days, telephoning with some exciting news. The mischief in his voice was unmistakable. "Don," he said, "how would you like to be an assistant to a questioned document examiner?"

I could almost see him smiling at my bewilderment as I stuttered, "A what?" Jacobs then went to explain that a questioned document examiner was a forensic scientist trained to examine all types of documentary evidence including suspected forgery of handwriting, typewriting, papers, inks, and charred documents, and to testify in court as an expert witness. Photography was used to both analyze and record documentary evidence and to make demonstration exhibits for court use.

I drew a complete blank when Jacobs identified Clark Sellers as the man who had advertised for an assistant. A few hours later when I did some investigations of my own, I learned about Sellers's nationwide fame as a questioned document examiner and expert witness. Among the cases in which he had testified with

27

dazzling effectiveness were the Winnie Ruth Judd trunk murder, the Hauptmann-Lindbergh kidnaping case, and many other high-profile cases of that era. Sellers was one of the early pioneers in the use of demonstrative evidence in court.

So it was with fear and trepidation that I appeared at Sellers's office door a few days later, fully expecting to be rejected as completely unqualified. Instead, to my astonishment, I was hired on the spot at the magnificent sum of $1.15 per hour. This was during the early World War II years when most able-bodied young men, including David Black, Sellers's former associate, had been drafted into the service. Sellers needed help badly. His new unlikely candidate with a 4F military service exemption came along just in the nick of time.

Finding My Niche:
I Am Catapulted Into the Field
of Questioned Documents and Mentor with
Three of Its Great Pioneers

Thus began my seven-year apprenticeship program, starting with five years in the Sellers office followed by one year in New York with Albert D. Osborn and finally concluding in Chicago with Herbert J. Walter. In terms of present-day academics, this kind of personal study would seem to be old-fashioned and impractical. Yet, that was the way many of us did it in the old days, and I am

Donald Doud, about 1941.

still convinced it was the best way. It was certainly better than the present-day practice of permitting teacher's assistants to teach college graduate studies. The reader will have an opportunity in a later chapter of this book to become better acquainted with the three mentors under whom I studied and to judge for themselves the value of apprenticeship training.

Having completed my self-directed training program and achieving somewhat of a reputation throughout the profession as a diligent, honest, and careful worker, I was invited by John F. Tyrrell of Milwaukee to associate with him as a partner, with the eventual goal of taking over his practice. Tyrrell was eighty-nine years old at the time and was held in high esteem by his fellow document examiners. He had pioneered in the development of sophisticated methods for examining handwriting, typewriting, and inks, and was known throughout the world for his work with charred document decipherment. The list of cases in which he had testified read like a Who's-Who of famous criminal trials, including the Mollineaux society poisoning, Rice-Patrick, the Hauptmann-Lindbergh kidnapping, State of Illinois vs. Leopold and Loeb, Heirens serial murder, and Allis Chalmers-CIO stuffed ballot case, all tried during the early part of the twentieth century.

A year had passed since our association—a year of generally uneventful collaboration in a firm now known as TYRRELL AND DOUD. But then a case came along that sent shock waves through our relationship. It involved former State Department official Alger Hiss, convicted of lying about his Communist activities, and his

30

motion for a new trial. Hiss needed a questioned document examiner to examine some typewritten documents for him, and it was I, and not my esteemed associate, who was selected to do the job.

3

Woodstock N230,099: The Typewriter That Convicted Alger Hiss

Did Whitaker Chambers Forge a Typewriter?

"I am confident that in the future the full facts showing how Chambers was able to carry out forgery by typewriter will be disclosed."

ALGER HISS, 1951

"Did you say *forgery by typewriter*?" I exploded into the ear of private investigator Raymond Schindler who was calling from New York. "Are you telling me that Alger Hiss claims someone forged the typewritten documents that sent him to prison for perjury?"

Sitting at his desk across the room from me, I could see a concerned look pass over the face of my octogenarian associate, John Tyrrell. He had overheard me mention the name of Alger Hiss and he didn't like it one bit. Gesturing vigorously with both hands, he made it quite clear that I should talk to him before committing myself to any examination for the man who had been convicted of betraying his country.

Tyrrell's reaction was not too surprising. Three years earlier, on April 3, 1948, citizens of the United States received some shocking news: Alger Hiss, protégé of President Franklin Roosevelt, former State Department official, representative of the American delegation at Yalta, and head of the Carnegie Endowment for International Peace, *was a Communist espionage agent*—at least that's what Whitaker Chambers claimed in his testimony before the House Un-American Activities Committee (HUAC). At a time when the nation was being traumatized by rumors of Russian Sputniks, Hollywood producers and actors with alleged Communist ties, and liberal politicians praising the virtues of Communist dictators, Chambers's allegations might just have been the straw that broke the camel's back.

But Whitaker Chambers's appearance before HUAC was far from impressive. A serious, heavy-set man in his late forties and one of the senior editors of *Time* magazine, Chambers appeared at the committee hearing wearing a rumpled old suit that looked like it had been slept in. Nor was his testimony much better as he hesitantly detailed his reasons for leaving the Communist apparatus in the late 1930s and, some ten years later, exposing Alger Hiss as a fellow member of the same espionage cell. Only a handful of HUAC members, including Richard Nixon, congressman from California, were impressed enough to subpoena him back for additional testimony.

All of that changed a few months later when Alger Hiss sued Chambers for slander. At a Baltimore deposition hearing on November 17, 1948, Chambers dramatically produced a large manila envelope containing sixty-five typewritten documents dated between January 5 and April 1, 1938, and four brief, handwritten memos. According to Chambers's testimony, the "Baltimore Documents," as they became known, were retyped copies of confidential State Department documents "borrowed" from State Department files by Hiss and copied on a typewriter used in the Hiss home. (Photocopying would have been a far better method, but that process wasn't available until some decades later.) After returning the originals, Hiss would customarily deliver the retyped copies to a courier for the Communist cell, of whom Chambers was one of the most active. In the case of the sixty-five Baltimore Documents, he had set them aside as an "insurance policy" against Communist retaliation when he finally decided to quit the party. The four handwritten memos, he believed, were written by Hiss, an assertion Hiss later admitted.

The most sensational aspect of Chambers's accusations involved the so-called "Pumpkin Papers." Armed with a subpoena from the HUAC, Chambers led committee members to a hollowed-out pumpkin on his farm containing five developed and undeveloped microfilms of additional State Department communiques. The bizarre nature of this evidence created an atmosphere of both intrigue and suspicion on the part of HUAC members. They looked more kindly on the sixty-five Baltimore Documents, which seemed to represent a more reliable way of judging the truth or falsity of Chambers's allegations.

Ramos Feehan, questioned document examiner for the FBI, compared the typewriting on the Baltimore Documents with the "Hiss Standards," correspondence of Priscilla Hiss (Alger Hiss's wife) from the 1930s, prepared on a Woodstock manual typewriter given to Priscilla by her father. Feehan reported that sixty-four of the sixty-five Baltimore Documents were typed on the Hiss typewriter, basing his identification on ten similarly scarred and out-of-alignment letters. The defects that individualized the work of this machine, Feehan explained, came about through wear and accidental damage to both the typebars and the type itself.

Attorneys for Hiss were made aware of Feehan's findings and apparently accepted Hiss's explanation that, somehow or other, Chambers had broken into his home to type the incriminating documents. Chambers's reason for doing so was not made clear, but apparently it was to frame Hiss with whom he had some disagreement.

The typewriter itself was no longer in Hiss's possession, and investigators for both the FBI and the Alger Hiss defense searched diligently to find it. Surprisingly, it was Hiss investigators who finally claimed victory. The typewriter had been given to the Hiss maid, apparently in late 1938, and had passed through several hands before ending up in the possession of a handyman by the name of Ira Lockey. It was a Woodstock typewriter of ancient vintage, and it was still in working order. The serial number stamped on the frame was N230,099.

Based primarily on Chambers's testimony and Feehan's typewriting evidence, Alger Hiss was finally indicted and brought to trial. Charged with two counts of perjury (the statutes had lapsed on the more serious charge of espionage), the first trial of Hiss resulted in a hung jury. The second trial, held in a different venue, resulted in Hiss's conviction. No doubt contributing to that verdict was the presence in the courtroom, throughout the trial, of Woodstock N230,099—introduced into evidence as the Hiss machine but never the subject of testimony by either prosecution or defense. Nevertheless, on closing argument, prosecutor Thomas F. Murray dramatically pointed to the old machine and said: "That typewriter sitting there is the immutable witness forever against Alger Hiss." In fact, nobody had ever identified N230,099 as having typed the Baltimore Documents. Feehan of the FBI had only testified to a connection between the Hiss Standards and the Baltimore Documents.

Hiss was ultimately sentenced to five years in Lewisburg Federal Penitentiary. At the time of Schindler's telephone call to me, he was still in prison with two more years to serve.

But confinement behind prison bars had not silenced Alger

Hiss, who continued to protest his innocence to fellow inmates and anyone else who would listen. Now working on evidence to support a motion for a new trial, Hiss sought help on the outside from friends and sympathizers, of whom there appeared to be an endless supply. One of the most tireless and innovative of these was New York attorney Chester Lane, who acted not only as Hiss's counsel but also as one of the chief exponents of a novel new theory mentioned only obliquely by Hiss at the time of his conviction—*forgery by typewriter*. According to Lane's hypotheses, Woodstock typewriter N230,099, found in the possession of handyman Ira Lockey, was not the true Alger Hiss typewriter but was, in fact, a fake created by Whitaker Chambers for the sole purpose of implicating Hiss in the espionage plot. This was an entirely new theory, not mentioned at either trial. Exactly how Chambers was able to substitute the fake Woodstock machine for Hiss's own typewriter was, at this point at least, left to the imagination.

Schindler's telephone call was one of the few times a prospective client had asked to speak to me personally rather than to my world-renowned associate. In addition, that client was, arguably, the world's most famous private investigator. Why did Schindler single me out to investigate Hiss's forgery-by-typewriter theory? "I had heard that you were somewhat of a specialist in Woodstock typewriter problems," Schindler later explained, "and based upon our personal acquaintanceship and your reputation in the field, I knew that you would 'call them the way you saw them' regardless of any outside pressures."

I first met Ray Schindler during my training period with Clark Sellers. Our paths crossed again when I worked in New York and Chicago, including one memorable meeting during my honeymoon when Schindler invited me and my new wife to a Chicago session of Erle Stanley Gardner's "Court of Last Resort". A stepchild of Gardner's "Perry Mason"[1] series and his intense interest in the criminal justice system, the Court of Last Resort[2] was composed of forensic, legal, and penal experts from all parts of the country who reviewed murder cases where it was suspected that a miscarriage of justice had taken place.

Anxious to impress my bride, I quickly accepted Schindler's invitation without asking about the case file to be reviewed. Unfortunately, it proved to be a particularly bloody murder and rape of a young woman, illustrated by color slides, in which forensic pathologist Dr. Richard Ford argued that the wrong man had been convicted. Later in our hotel room, I was faced with the task of reassuring my dismayed companion that questioned document examination was different from forensic pathology and

---

1. "Perry Mason", 1957-1966 (271 episodes), CBS Television, Producer Thomas Cornwall Jackson.

2. Gardner, with many of his investigative, forensic, and legal friends, spent hundreds of hours on a project he called "The Court of Last Resort". The goal of the project was to review and, as appropriate, to reverse, miscarriages of justice against criminal defendants who were convicted owing to poor original legal representation or especially to the abuse or misinterpretation of medical and other forensic evidence.

involved no bloodshed whatsoever. My answer must have been reassuring because we are still together after more than fifty years, three children, and seven grandchildren. Regrettably, Dick Ford committed suicide at a fairly young age, perhaps unable to bear any more of the blood and death he was forced to witness.

Ray Schindler could easily have been mistaken for a traveling salesman, judging by his jovial manner and the number of people in all parts of the United States he knew by their first names. Yet, there was another side to this American-style Sherlock Holmes. When investigating a crime, he changed into a bloodhound on the scent—single-minded and tenacious to a fault—always searching for more clues to aid him in reaching a conclusion. In the Bahamas murder trial of Sir Harry Oakes, as one example, Schindler made forensic science history and helped free a wrongfully accused defendant when he proved to the satisfaction of the judge that a fingerprint of Count de Marigny's that purportedly appeared on a wooden screen at the side of Sir Harry's bed was a fraud. Using a rubber lift-off material, an over-zealous detective hired by the Duke of Windsor had removed a fingerprint of de Marigny's from an entirely different object, the surface of which, according to Schindler's devastating testimony, was circular in pattern rather than ridged like the wood grain on Sir Harry's screen. I couldn't help but wonder whether Schindler was on the trail of similar skullduggery by Whitaker Chambers.

It was nothing that dramatic, said Schindler in a visit to Milwaukee a few days after his phone call. "All I am in the Hiss case is a babysitter and an errand boy." This humorous characterization was typical of Schindler, who liked to portray himself as a common man who always found himself in the right place at the right time. Nevertheless, there was a grain of truth to what he said. In fact, one of Schindler's assignments, so he told me, was to keep his eye on a young attorney working for the Alger Hiss defense team, apparently to keep him from falling under some perceived Marxist influence. Schindler's employer, oddly enough, was a prominent New York law firm working in the interest of the young man's father. Perhaps it was symptomatic of the anti-Communist hysteria that gripped the country at this time that a father worried about his son's association with Alger Hiss would employ the most famous investigator in America to perform a simple task more suited to some obscure private detective. Even more astonishing, the defense team apparently knew of Schindler's conflicting role of working on Hiss's behalf while at the same time tailing one of his own attorneys. Schindler's other assignments, he hastened to reassure Tyrrell and me, would demand more of his investigative skills, including trying to ferret out Woodstock typewriter information from reluctant sources.

Schindler strode back and forth in front of Tyrrell's massive desk and, uncharacteristically, answered our questions in monosyllables. I could tell that he was having difficulty explaining the details of Chester Lane's forgery-by-typewriter theory. He obviously didn't want to stick his neck out describing something to Tyrrell and me that attorney Chester Lane might later contradict.

Yet, I couldn't accept employment without knowing precisely what my role in the case would be. Outspoken as always, my octogenarian associate blurted out, "Mr. Schindler, I can tell you right now, Mr. Doud is not about to accept employment in this case until he knows exactly what is expected of him. If you can't tell us, perhaps there is someone who can." I would have put it more tactfully, but I was secretly grateful to my feisty old partner for taking me off the hook.

Never one to let a misunderstanding get in the way of progress, the world's most famous private eye picked up the phone, dialed a New York number he had stored somewhere in his head, and arranged for Chester Lane, Alger Hiss's right-hand man, to come to Milwaukee to tell us all about it.

The following week two distinguished visitors from New York arrived at the Tyrrell-Doud offices in Milwaukee and sat down at our large walnut conference table. John Tyrrell, still bothered by what he conceived to be some hidden agenda behind the activities of Schindler and Lane, nevertheless got caught up in the excitement and intrigue surrounding Hiss's forgery-by-typewriter theory. He decided to join in the fray and try to keep his young associate out of trouble.

Ray Schindler, dressed informally in a plaid sports coat stretched at the seams from keeping his prominent midriff under control, was his usual friendly, talkative self—in a hurry, as before, to get things moving. His companion, Chester Lane, was the exact opposite. Slender, tall, and conservatively dressed in British tweeds, his manner was unhurried, unsmiling, and to the point. Alger Hiss was framed by Whitaker Chambers, said Lane, there was no question about that. And, if I decided to accept employment by them, I would find out the same thing. Noticing my look of apprehension at this outburst, Schindler broke into the conversation and reassured Tyrrell and me that the Hiss defense expected nothing but an objective, scientific examination of typewriter evidence and would accept the outcome whether it was favorable or unfavorable to their theory. "Ah, yes, yes," said Lane, realizing that his remarks had caused us some concern, "we only want the truth—the same thing you would say under oath if you were testifying in court."

Tyrrell and I then listened in fascination as Lane described the details of Hiss's forgery-by-typewriter theory and what steps the Hiss team had taken, or were planning to take, to determine whether or not they could prove it.

The first question we asked ourselves, said Lane, was, 'Is it possible to construct a forged typewriter that would embody in its work the same identifying typeface flaws as those found in a second typewriter?' Unfortunately, we could find no ready answer to that question, either in the literature or in any experimental work by others. We, therefore, went about supplying our own answer—in the only way possible—by hiring someone to try it out.

Chester Lane's own words, appearing in the transcript of Hiss's motion for a new trial, describe the origin, progress, and eventual results of an unusual experiment to clone a typewriter and, in the process, try to win a new trial for Alger Hiss.

We now believed that Chambers had in some way forged the Baltimore Documents so as to make them appear to have been written on the Hiss typewriter. I decided to explore this possibility—to see whether a typewriter could be created which would duplicate a sufficient number of the peculiar characteristics of another to meet the tests which as applied by Mr. Feehan (the Government expert) had satisfied him that the same machine had been used in this case for the two sets of documents. If this—which so far as I know had never before been generally supposed possible—could be done, the demonstration of it would, it seemed to me, neutralize the 'scientific' evidence which had been necessary to corroborate Chambers's testimony and which hence had been vital to the government's case.

Accordingly, I consulted one Martin K. Tytell, a noted typewriter engineer in New York City, and explained my problem to him. I asked whether, without ever seeing the typewriter in evidence in the Hiss case—Woodstock N230,099—but working simply from sample documents typed on that machine, he could make another typewriter which would produce typed documents so similar in peculiar typing characteristics to the sample as to meet the tests of identity applied by Mr. Feehan. He said that not only could he do that, but he believed that he could make a machine the product of which would be so exactly similar in all respects—not merely in the ten or so characters analyzed by Mr. Feehan—that no expert could distinguish documents typed on the two machines, even if put on his guard by warning in advance that a deliberate effort had been made to construct a duplicate machine. Of course, he said, an expert not so forewarned (as Mr. Feehan was probably not forewarned) would be even more likely to be mistaken in his attempted identification.

At my request Mr. Tytell undertook to try to create such a machine. The machine he built is now in my possession and, as his affidavit shows, it was constructed solely from samples of typing on the alleged Hiss machine (N230,099). Neither he nor anyone working with him had been allowed at any time to inspect the machine which he was attempting to duplicate, or to take impressions of the original type on it.

Tytell's own affidavit described his visits to typewriter shops in various parts of the country where he searched for Woodstock parts of the same vintage as N230,099 and having similar wear characteristics. Finally, in a tedious trial-and-error process that took him over one year to complete, Tytell carved imperfections into the typeface metal with engraving tools, bent and reshaped the typebars, and fitted and refitted them into the body or "segment" portion of the reconstituted machine. As the work progressed, Lane submitted samples of the typewriting to a Boston expert for her suggestions on how the forgeries could be improved.

Near the end of the project, an expert in "typographic forgeries" formerly associated with Harvard University's Fogg Museum was consulted for fine tuning of the results. In the end, despite Tytell's

adoption of the suggested changes, both experts had to admit they could still distinguish between the work of the forged machine and that of Woodstock N230,099. Nevertheless, both claimed in their affidavits,

Martin K. Tytell, New York typewriter engineer.

"If not forewarned, most questioned document examiners would pronounce the two to be the same." What a strange caveat to put into an affidavit.

During a break for lunch, Chester Lane candidly admitted to Tyrrell and me that despite his expert's optimistic evaluation of Tytell's typewriter forgery, the results probably did not reach the level of proof required by an appeals court. They demonstrated only that it was possible to do an acceptable job of forging a typewriter, and who was to say that Whitaker Chambers couldn't have done better?

A few weeks later when I finally had an opportunity to examine the same documents, my reaction was even less favorable. After about two hours of microscopic comparisons, I was readily able to separate Tytell's forgeries from the known typewriting and felt I could have done so whether "forewarned" or not. Lane did not ask for a report on my examination. The two Boston experts had conceded that the forgery was not perfect, and a report from still a third expert would have been redundant.

Back in the Tyrrell-Doud offices following our lunch break, I could detect a hint of excitement in Lane's voice as he described the events leading up to the second and most important part of Hiss's forgery-by-typewriter theory. His investigators had discovered an apparent discrepancy between the time Woodstock N230,099 was manufactured and the history of documents supposedly typed on it. Chambers, it would appear, had selected the *wrong model* of Woodstock for his forgeries of the Baltimore

Documents. No one ever disputed that fact that, upon his retirement in 1932, Thomas Fansler, a Northwestern Mutual Life general agent from Philadelphia, gave his daughter Priscilla Hiss a Woodstock typewriter formerly used in his office. Priscilla subsequently used the typewriter in the Hiss home for correspondence (including the Hiss Standards) until the typewriter was given away in the late 1930s to the Hiss maid. But, according to Lane, N230,099 could not possibly have been that typewriter. It wasn't manufactured until two years *after* Fansler first purchased his Woodstock. Lane was sure of his facts—he had gotten them straight from the horse's mouth.

The most reliable source of typewriter serial number information is usually to be found in records of the manufacturer—in this case the R. C. Allen Office Machines, Inc., successor to The Woodstock Typewriter Company. Joseph Schmitt, factory manager under both regimes, reported to Hiss investigators that, based upon production figures available to him, Woodstock N230,099 would have been manufactured in July, or perhaps August, of 1929. Woodstock records did not permit a more precise date of manufacture.

Standing alone, the July or August 1929 dates meant little, but when compared to another date, 1927, when Thomas Fansler allegedly purchased the Woodstock in question for use in his insurance office, it had the kick of a mule. If not manufactured by Woodstock until July 1929 at the earliest, how was it possible for typewriter N230,099 to have been used to type documents in the

Fansler office as early as 1927? It was not, said Lane. But there was something missing. How did they know for sure when Fansler's Woodstock was first purchased? The answer came through interviews in Philadelphia with former Fansler employees and from Thomas Grady, the local Woodstock agency salesman who originally sold Fansler the typewriter.

Still living in Philadelphia when interviewed by Hiss investigators, Grady proved to be a provocative witness. Despite the passage of some twenty years, he distinctly remembered selling a Woodstock typewriter to Fansler's insurance agency "in early 1927." The Woodstock sales agency had destroyed sales invoices for that year, but he knew it couldn't be any later than 1927 because he quit the company in December of 1927. The Woodstock agency (the only one authorized to sell Woodstocks in Philadelphia) was more successful in locating sales invoices running from early 1928 through 1932. They failed to find any record of a Woodstock typewriter being sold to the Fansler office during this period of time.

The 1927 date was likewise confirmed by interviews with H. L. Martin, who sold insurance from the Fansler office, and by a former secretary who did the typing for both Fansler and Martin. Both stated unequivocally that only one typewriter was ever purchased from the Woodstock sales agency in Philadelphia and that was a new Woodstock sold to the company in early 1927 when Fansler first went into business. They also recalled that upon his retirement in 1932, Fansler took this same Woodstock typewriter home as a gift to Priscilla Hiss, his daughter.

Armed with helpful affidavits from his Philadelphia connections, Chester Lane now searched for and found a final source of evidence that he hoped would nail the lid on the coffin. It consisted of documents from the files of Northwestern Mutual Life Insurance Company (NML) of Milwaukee, Fansler's home office. Responding to Chester Lane's request for typewritten correspondence originating in the Fansler office, NML indicated that they had found twelve letters, all dated during the critical 1927 to 1930 period. Reluctant to turn the correspondence over to Hiss investigators with whom they had experienced some difficulty, NML readily agreed to submit them to the firm of Tyrrell and Doud whose senior partner they knew well. He had formerly headed up their new policy division.

Now reassured that I would be dealing with documentary evidence from a verifiable source and under no pressure from Chester Lane to slant my findings one way or the other, I decided to accept employment in the Alger Hiss case. Tyrrell reluctantly gave his approval to the venture.

Delivered to the Tyrrell-Doud office by a Northwestern Mutual Life courier, the twelve letters were now joined by a host of other documents, both originals and photocopies, disgorged from Chester Lane's briefcase. I can still remember the feelings of excitement and perhaps a little apprehension as I took my first look at the documents that had helped convict Hiss and, according to one news commentator, "forever changed the course of history." Included were several of the retyped State Department communiques (Baltimore Documents) and the so-called Hiss Standards, correspondence typed by Priscilla Hiss on the Woodstock typewriter given to her by her father. For the moment at least, the twelve Fansler documents would be the principal focus of my examination. They appeared to hold the key to the history of a typewriter that allegedly journeyed from Fansler's insurance office to the home of Priscilla Hiss and finally into the hands of handyman Ira Lockey—but in the end, according to Lane, not as the original Hiss machine but as an alleged forgery.

As Lane and Schindler prepared to leave our office for the return trip to New York, Lane turned and said, "I talked to Mr. Hiss shortly before coming here, and he wants to reiterate what Schindler said earlier—that you are expected to call them exactly the way you see them, whether favorable or unfavorable to our interests. But he also wants you to bear in mind that there may be obstacles placed in your path by those who conspire to keep him from achieving final vindication."

After the two men had left, John Tyrrell snorted, "Now what in blazes did Lane mean by that statement?" Then, bad eyesight and all, my octogenarian friend pulled out his three-power magnifier and took his first look at the Baltimore Documents and the Hiss Standards that were so important in convicting Alger Hiss of perjury. I could hardly wait to get started on the twelve documents sent by the Thomas Fansler Agency to NML. Lane was relying on them to provide the scientific evidence necessary to support his forgery-by-typewriter theory, and I was there to ascertain the truth—whether or not it agreed with Lane's theory.

At the time the Fansler documents were written in the late 1920s and early 1930s, there were five major manufacturers of typewriters in the United States: Remington, Royal, Underwood, L. C. Smith, and Woodstock (IBM came at a later time). The typewriters they manufactured, and continued to manufacture until electric typewriters and computers took over, were manual machines of a common typebar construction (with the type being soldered to the ends of long thin bars). Yet, each one had its own distinguishing features, including the design of its type of "typestyle." Model changes were frequently made, usually accompanied by changes in typestyle, some involving only a few letters or numerals, others the complete font. The Woodstock Company made many changes throughout the years including one that proved to be of vital importance to my examination of the Hiss documents.

With our visitors on their way back to New York and John Tyrrell taking his usual afternoon nap at the Milwaukee Athletic Club, I finally had an opportunity to get down to my examination of the twelve Fansler documents.

The dates on the documents, I discovered, covered a period running from July of 1927 to February of 1930. The July 1927 document was clearly typed on a Woodstock machine and, in point of time, was entirely consistent with Thomas Grady's statement about selling Fansler a Woodstock several months earlier.

The Typewriter That Convicted Alger Hiss

Examining the July 1927 and subsequent documents in date order, I searched the letters and numerals for similarities or differences in the style of Woodstock type used, and on one document after another I found the type design to be identical. I had been working for over four hours and had examined the typewriting on only six of the documents. My eyes were getting tired and so was I. I wanted to quit but decided to struggle through one more examination.

Suddenly I was jolted out of my lethargy. There under my microscope was a document dated July 8, 1929, differing in typestyle from the earlier ones. Now wide awake, I carefully examined the letters and numerals on the next five documents, ending with one dated February 3, 1930. The typestyle agreed perfectly with the July 8, 1929 typewriting, but differed from that on the earlier documents beginning with July 1927. *Two* different Woodstocks must have been used in the Fansler office!

So much for the statements of three individuals and a typewriter agency from Philadelphia that *only one* Woodstock was purchased by the Fansler Agency during this period of time. So much also for the alleged anachronism between the July 1927 date of the first letter and the July or August 1929 manufacturing time that factory manager Schmitt had placed on Woodstock N230,099.

Equally important, the typewriting from the second Fansler Woodstock, and not the first, matched the typestyle of N230,099, the Hiss Standards, and the Baltimore Documents.

When I provided this information to Chester Lane, he now

came up with a new forgery-by-typewriter theory. How could a typewriter made by Woodstock in July or August of 1929 have been packaged, shipped, and delivered to Fansler's Philadelphia office in time to type the July 8, 1929, document to NML? It couldn't, said Lane. Even if one were to assume that N230,099 was manufactured on July 1st of 1929, the shipping and delivery time alone would have taken almost two weeks. The logic of Lane's position was unassailable, but again all depended upon factory manager Schmitt's dating of the serial number. Fortunately, I knew of another way of placing approximate dates on typewriting that, if I was lucky, might confirm or reject Schmitt's findings.

Most questioned document examiners of my day maintained extensive files of typewriting information that they continually updated, at least on a yearly basis. My records pretty much started in the 1940s when I first entered the profession. However, John Tyrrell's ran back to the very beginnings of the typewriter industry, including early records of the Woodstock Typewriter Company. I had not been employed in any case requiring use of Tyrrell's typewriting files and had no idea how systematically they had been maintained. But when I finally dragged the musty old records out of a file drawer and carefully reviewed them, I could have kissed my old associate. There on file cards, yellowed around the edges, were two neatly scripted notations accompanied by actual typewriting specimens. The first one, obtained from the local Woodstock typewriter agency, provided dates of "1919 to early 1926" for manufacture of the model of typewriter used for the first six Fansler documents beginning with July 1927. Thomas Grady apparently sold Fansler in 1927 a typewriter model discontinued in 1926.

The next notation contained information most damaging to Lane's forgery-by-typewriter theory, or so I thought. It concerned the typestyle of the second Fansler Woodstock and the July 8, 1929, and subsequent documents prepared on it. "This style of type was manufactured from late 1926 to late 1928 or early 1929" the notation read. And clipped to the file card were actual specimens of type of 1926, 1927, and 1928 obtained from the Milwaukee Woodstock agency. The "early" 1929 termination date to the typestyle undoubtedly referred to the first quarter—it certainly did not describe anything as late as July 1929. Then I ran across reference to a "new action" of Woodstock typewriter being introduced in "March of 1929." A mechanical change of this magnitude would certainly have signaled a typestyle change as well.

At the least, Tyrrell's records had now placed a time period of "1926 to early 1929" for the manufacture of Fansler's second typewriter. Insofar as Lane's new forgery-by-typewriter theory was concerned, it didn't matter when during that period Fansler purchased his second Woodstock. It would have arrived in his Philadelphia office in plenty of time to have typed the July 8, 1929, letter.

Chester Lane's reaction to this information was the exact opposite of my own. "This represents further proof," he said, "that

N230,099 is a fabricated machine. The July or August 1929 date of its manufacture, as reported by Schmitt of Woodstock, is in direct conflict with the period between 1926 and early 1929 when your records indicate a typestyle of this kind was in production. The typestyle and the serial number don't match!" Lane's reasoning on this point didn't make much sense to me. But apparently he was saying that Whitaker Chambers, while assembling his "forged" typewriter, got the parts of two different models of scavenged Woodstocks mixed up—one containing the serial number N230,099 and the other the 1926 to early 1929 type font.

I responded to Lane's unusual interpretation of the evidence in a letter dated January 8, 1952:

> The specimens from typewriter N230,099 and the NML documents [dated July 1929 and later] as well as the Hiss Standards and the Baltimore Documents were all written on the same *model* typewriter. Obviously then, if they show the same typeface design, all of them including typewriter N230,099 were manufactured during the same date period which would appear to be 1926, 1927, 1928 or early 1929. Wouldn't the logical assumption then be that Mr. Schmitt was wrong in his statement about approximately July or August 1929? Certainly N230,099 would not be manufactured during a period when a new and different model was being put into production.

With Lane still clinging tenaciously to Schmitt's dating of N230,099 and I to the typestyle dating from Tyrrell's files, the two of us finally were able to reach agreement on one point. I needed to compare the typewriting from the second Fansler Woodstock with the Hiss Standards to make absolutely sure that the *same* Woodstock typewriter was used. Nothing could just be assumed in this strange case. With all the ambiguous testimony coming out of Philadelphia, who was to say that Fansler might not have acquired still a third Woodstock typewriter that was subsequently given to Priscilla Hiss.

Up to this point I had been dealing with typestyles and typestyle changes in Woodstocks manufactured during certain periods of time. Now I was being asked to search for scarred and out-of-alignment characters in the Hiss Standards and Fansler documents that might or might not identify them as being written on identically the same typewriter.

Trying to resolve this problem involved an entirely different set of circumstances than the one facing questioned document examiner Feeshan of the FBI when he compared the Hiss Standards with the Baltimore Documents. Those were dated around the same time. I was being asked to compare typewritings based upon the *evolution* of typeface defects over a period of some eight years—a most unusual and difficult task.

The defects that occur in type through extended use of a typewriter are similar, in some respects, to the dings, stains, and rattles that gradually develop in one's own car and then continue on in increasing intensity when you give it to your college-bound son or daughter. If he or she then invites you out for a ride on a Sunday afternoon, you may be pretty sure the car you are riding in was once your own, but the additional dings, fabric stains, and rattles may make you wonder whether you could prove it if you had to.

So it was with the documents from the second Fansler Woodstock. Apparently written on a fairly new typewriter, I spent a considerable amount of time trying to trace the incipient defects of the 1929 and 1930 Fansler typewriting through the Hiss Standards prepared two to eight years later. Although not asked to do so, I also felt obligated to include the Baltimore Documents in the examination. My report to Lane outlined the work I did, to try to resolve this unique problem.

A comparison of the individual typeface characteristics in the Fansler typewritings, dated July 8, 1929 and after, with the Baltimore letters and Hiss Standards, shows a tendency, in the 1929-1930 Fansler specimens, toward the development of typeface defects that later became so highly identifying in the 1933 and 1935 Hiss Standards and in the Baltimore Letters. For instance, in 1929, the Fansler documents were typed on a machine that was apparently quite new and had not as yet developed many defective characters. However, even in those early days, such defects as the *u* with the bent right serif, the *o* printing heavier on the right, the *a* printing heavier on the bottom, and the *I* printing below the baseline, were manifest. In 1930 the *d* became defective at the lower right serif and in 1931 the *e* appears to have been damaged on the lower right extension. The extensive scar on the right side of the lower loop to the *g* appears to have occurred between 1931 [the date of the Hiss standard to Miss Hellings] and 1935 [the date of the letter subsequently addressed to Walter L. Tibbetts]. This scar is found in all subsequently dated documents. I can find no evidence to show that these early Fansler documents from July 8, 1929 to Feb. 14, 1930 *could not* have been written on the same typewriter used for the Baltimore Letters and the Hiss Standards.

Although concluding with a negative inference that fell somewhat short of positive proof, I had shed some light on an important part of the evidence. Starting with the July 8, 1929, letter, I had established a chain of evidence from the Fansler letters through the Hiss Standards up to the time the Hiss family gave the typewriter away to their maid. My inclusion of the Baltimore Documents in the identification didn't seem to bother Lane at all. "This proves they are forgeries," he said. "Woodstock N230,099 wasn't in existence at the time their progenitor, the July 8, 1929, Fansler letter, was written." But again, everything about Lane's theory depended upon the accuracy of Schmitt about Woodstock's serial number information production date.

In 1951 and 1952, at the time of my examination of the Hiss problem, over twenty years had passed since the manufacture of Woodstock N230,099. The records of the Woodstock Company, never very reliable, were transferred to a new entity, R. C. Allen. Even before the change, strange things were happening—serial numbers were skipped, sometimes in large blocks, monthly dates were not assigned to production figures, and records of serial numbers stamped on individual machines were either lost or not kept at all. After the merger, the record keeping continued to deteriorate. Even factory manager Schmitt and J. T. Carlson, vice president in charge of manufacturing, seemed baffled by contradictions in the Woodstock records. At one point, Carlson drafted an affidavit for Lane stating that N230,099 was likely produced in April or May of 1929, but later retracted that statement, saying it was based on research by a clerk. Schmitt equivocated between July and August of 1929, but tentatively settled on the earlier date.

I knew Schmitt personally and wrote to him at Woodstock requesting an interview to see whether I could help unearth records that might resolve the questions of when N230,099 was made. He politely refused my request, saying that both Carlson and he had already been visited several times by the FBI and Hiss investigators and there was simply no other Woodstock dating information available to them. It would appear that even Ray Schindler, with all of his persuasive powers, could not again gain entre to Woodstock Company records. In the end, to Chester Lane's shock and surprise,

Schmitt declined to sign an affidavit certifying to *any* date of manufacture.

Chester Lane claimed in his own affidavit to the court that Schmitt's refusal to sign an affidavit was just one more example of roadblocks placed in the way of Alger Hiss and his effort to obtain "final vindication." I think Schmitt's reasons were more altruistic. He did not sign an affidavit because he was still in doubt about the time when N230,099 was made.

Insofar as I was concerned, there were only two final questions to be answered. Was FBI expert Feehan on firm footing when he identified the Baltimore Documents and the Hiss Standards as being typed on the same typewriter? And secondly, a question not posed to Feehan: Was *that* typewriter Woodstock N230,099?

I started by comparing the typewriting on the Baltimore Documents with the Hiss Standards, admittedly typed on Priscilla Hiss's Woodstock machine. I had previously conducted this same examination during my studies of the Fansler documents but wanted to review them one more time, and, as before, I found the same scarred, poorly aligned, and "off-their-feet" characters in both sets of documents. Equally important, the remainder of the letters and numerals were free of significant defects, thus establishing a negative as well as a positive aspect to the evidence. FBI expert Feehan was right in his testimony at the trial. The Hiss Standards and the Baltimore Documents were typed on the same Woodstock typewriter; there was just no doubt about it.

I next compared the typewriting on the Hiss Standards and the

Baltimore Documents with specimens prepared on Woodstock
N230,099. The identifying typeface characteristics matched
perfectly, and the other letters and numerals were free of significant
flaws. For Whitaker Chambers or someone else to have so perfectly
forged a typewriter incorporating both aspects of its identifying
features was, in my judgment, an impossibility.

Notwithstanding the results of my examinations, Lane still
insisted that I assemble parts of my reports into the form of an
affidavit. Reflecting back on the conflict between my dating of
N230,099 by typestyle and Schmitt's by Woodstock records, I
finally decided it would be unwise to do so. It was not what I had
discovered about the typewriting that bothered me, it was what
interpretations Lane might place upon that evidence. If I were
forced to appear in court to validate my affidavit, as by law I must
do, I would be placed in an absolutely untenable position. On
January 13, 1952, in my final communication with Lane, I wrote:

> In your letter of January 9, 1952, you asked me to
> submit an affidavit on two unrelated points with which
> you hope to establish the theory that typewriter
> N230,099 was a fraudulently made up machine in
> support of the Government's case against Alger Hiss.
> I have worked conscientiously and diligently on this
> matter, but no evidence I have gathered to date has
> given me any reason to believe that theory, and I
> cannot subscribe to any statement tending to imply that
> evidence I have gathered supports that conclusion.

Thus ended my part in the Hiss-Chambers case. Like Schmitt and others who refused to sign affidavits, I was condemned in Lane's motion for a new trial as being fearful of repercussions from Hoover of the FBI or, by implication, the extreme anti-Communist element from the right. In fact, no one other than those working for Hiss ever contacted me in any way. I "called them the way I saw them," but Alger Hiss and his attorney Chester Lane were unwilling to accept my conclusions.

Whether Raymond Schindler suffered a similar castigation for his inability to help Hiss's cause I never did find out. Several years later when my wife and I visited him on the Hudson River estate of the Duchess de Tallyrand, I jokingly accused him of again acting as an "errand boy" and "babysitter", this time for the Duchess. (In fact, his role was a far more serious one of investigating threats against her and acting as her bodyguard.)

In the end, those of us who refused to sign affidavits for Alger Hiss were not the only ones unable to support Lane's forgery-by-typewriter theory. In his final ruling on Lane's motion for a new trial, Judge Henry Goddard summed up his opinion in two succinct paragraphs:

> The defense reasoning that N230,099 was manufactured after the Hiss machine is not sustained by any proof. Their theory is based wholly upon incomplete records from which they have drawn speculations from approximate dates of manufacture.

Some of their own witnesses cannot support their theory.

In the absence of any proof and in view of the many improbabilities in the theory of the defense, a jury could not reasonably find that Chambers constructed a duplicate typewriter or that N230,099 is not the Hiss machine.

The Motion is Denied

In 1978, after gaining access to FBI and prosecution records through the Freedom of Information Act, Hiss made his final legal effort to gain a new trial. Known as Petition for a Writ of Error Coram Nobis, the District Court for the Southern District of New York ruled against Alger Hiss, and all of his legal remedies were now exhausted.

Undeterred by this succession of defeats, Alger Hiss continued to proclaim his innocence to any and all who would listen. At one time he became quite popular as a lecturer at universities around the country, especially those with a liberal bent. Several books by others and two or three by Hiss himself were published with modest success. All of them took me to task for my unwillingness to sign an affidavit giving support to the forgery-by-typewriter theory.

But there was still one final chapter to be written.

Epilogue—Was "Ales" Alger?
Decrypted Soviet Cables—
The Smoking Gun?

1996 was not a good year for Alger Hiss. In March, news broke of a series of intercepted wartime Soviet cables, decrypted by the US Army Signal Corps and released to the public by the National Security Agency (NSA). From the standpoint of the Alger Hiss case, the most devastating of the lot was a March 30, 1945, cable from Antoli Gromov, the KGB station chief in Washington, D. C., to his Moscow comrades. The cable reported on a conversation between Iskhak A. Akhemerov, considered the most dangerous Soviet agent in the U. S., and a fellow spy whose code name was "Ales."

While NSA was reluctant to definitely identify Alger Hiss as being "Ales" (they said he *probably* was), everything in the cable points in that direction. It also confirms in important respects many of Whitaker Chambers' statements. "Ales" was a State Department official who had worked continuously for the GRU (Soviet military intelligence) since 1935. He was a member of the U. S. diplomatic team at Yalta and immediately following the meeting went to Moscow to receive a decoration from Andre Vyshinsky, USSR deputy foreign minister. These activities and others mentioned in the cables were unique to Alger Hiss and no other person.

In his 1990 memoir, *KGB: The Inside Story*,[1] ex-KGB Col. Oleg Gordievsky stated unequivocally that "Ales" was the code name for Alger Hiss. Mr. Gordievsky did not have access to the decrypted Soviet cables at the time he wrote the book. Was it just a coincidence that he too identified Alger Hiss as "Ales"?

After seeking vindication for more than fifty years, Alger Hiss died in November of 1996, still proclaiming his innocence.

---

1. Christopher Andrew and Oleg Gordievsky, *KGB: The Inside Story of Its Foreign Operations from Lenin to Gorbachev* (New York: Harper, 1990).

4

Branching Out

I Establish a Chicago Office
and Meet Fred Inbau,
a Scientific Evidence Icon

Much to John Tyrrell's surprise, my involvement in the Alger Hiss case did not destroy the reputation of the Tyrrell-Doud partnership but, in fact, enhanced it. Indeed, for a while I was deluged with requests from bar associations, service clubs, and law schools in Wisconsin to give slide lectures on the Hiss case. While these appearances may have educated the audiences and honed my abilities as a speaker, they did little to bring in new business, a critical need for a sluggish practice suffering from too few clients and too little income. With John Tyrrell about to retire and my growing family to support, I needed to expand my practice to a larger metropolitan area where there were many lawyers, lots of business activity, and frequent epidemics of crime and political corruption. Ninety miles to the south was that big, bad, boisterous city of Chicago which fit the description perfectly.

When I told my good friend and mentor, Herbert J. Walter, of my plans to establish a practice in the Chicago area, he was delighted. "We need you down here, Don," he said, "and I can help you get started." Walter went on to explain that the caseload in his office was more than he could handle, and he would try to direct certain clients to me rather than have them end up with "those ruddy charlatans up the street," as he referred to his largely graphological competitors.

Thus began a forty-year period of commuting from Milwaukee to Chicago by train, first on a once-a-week basis and finally two or three days a week as I gradually increased my business and established a permanent business address. Those were hectic times, and I can recall literally galloping the half mile from Union Station to my office on the 17th floor of the Temple Building in order to keep some appointment or to get ready for testimony in court. My old doctors at Barlow Sanatorium probably would have been horrified at my frenetic activity during those years, but I somehow or other managed to survive the fast pace of Chicago life and to actually thrive on it, physically.

In March of 1951, a meeting was held in Chicago that had a profound effect upon my future as a questioned document examiner. The American Academy of Forensic Sciences, a newly organized group of about one hundred forensic scientists (it has a membership today of almost five thousand), was holding its third annual meeting at the Drake Hotel in Chicago. Composed of seven sections—pathology, immunology, toxicology, psychiatry, police science, jurisprudence, and questioned documents—I had been invited by the program chairman to give a fifteen-minute presentation on questioned document examination. But he neglected to tell me that my talk was scheduled to take place in the Grand Ballroom of the Drake Hotel and that my audience was to be the entire membership of the academy, not just one section.

Shaking like a leaf, I gazed into the faces of this erudite group of forensic scientists, wondering whether they would sympathize with my plight if I lost my voice or forgot what I was going to say. But my fears were unfounded, and somehow or other I managed to do a fairly acceptable job of explaining the scope of questioned document work to an audience obviously intrigued with a forensic science specialty so different from their own.

As I stepped down from the speaker's platform, an energetic man of about forty with an ingratiating smile and an enviable crop of black hair (I was worried about losing mine) approached me with outstretched hand. "My name is Fred Inbau," he said. "I am a professor at Northwestern University Law School and would like to invite you to lecture at one of my scientific evidence classes if you are interested." Was I interested? You bet I was! The opportunity of talking to a group of budding young lawyers about my field of expertise was one that I would not miss for the world. But who was Fred Inbau? Where had I heard that name before? When I asked that same question of H. J. Walter a few hours later,

I was literally bowled over with what he had to say. Fred Inbau, it turned out, was the John Henry Wigmore Professor of Law (Emeritus) at Northwestern University Law School. Wigmore was a powerful figure in the legal community, and for Inbau to be chosen as his successor was a great honor. In his first years at the University, Fred Inbau had likewise established himself as a worldwide authority on scientific evidence and had pioneered the use of sophisticated interrogation techniques to evaluate the truth or falsity of statements made in criminal or civil cases. Inbau's books on the subject have been adopted as standard texts by law schools through the country. At an earlier time, Inbau was a member of Northwestern University's Scientific Crime Detection Laboratory and became its first director when the laboratory was sold to the Chicago police department. This concept of an all-inclusive crime detection laboratory was the precursor of virtually all other similar facilities in the United States, including the FBI laboratory in Washington, D. C. At the time of our first meeting, Inbau was chairman of the Jurisprudence Section of the American Academy of Forensic Sciences and was in line to become its fifth president.

This chance meeting with Fred Inbau at the Drake Hotel led to a forty-year friendship and involvement in countless classes and programs he headed up at Northwestern University Law School. It also led, indirectly, to Fred's marriage to a charming woman connected with the Chicago Art Institute, introduced to him by my wife Jane, an artist as well as a matchmaker.

Donald Doud, about 1956.

Inbau was not your usual type of university professor. Rather than lecturing endlessly to students of his scientific evidence classes, he invited forensic science specialists from various parts of the country to show them what the real world of crime investigation was all about. He also set up moot court demonstrations, of which I was occasionally a part, in which Inbau was the judge and his students acted as lawyers (or inquisitors, as the case might be) for the prosecution and defense. This practical interplay with students was probably more edifying to me than it was to them.

When Northwestern University Law School obtained a Ford Foundation grant to put on scientific evidence seminars for prosecutors and defense attorneys, Fred continued to draw on the expertise of specialists in all branches of the forensic sciences. My good friend Ordway Hilton, a questioned document examiner from New York, usually ended up lecturing to the prosecutors and I to the defense attorneys. The members of my group, I secretly felt, were the more interesting—at least they were the more argumentative and irascible. On more than one occasion I found myself at the center of diatribes about "that damn questioned document examiner for the government putting my innocent client away on flimsy evidence." In the two or three cases where they actually showed me the evidence, I was forced to admit that the government experts were probably right.

Don't Cry for Me Adjmis:
A Tearful Tale of Wealthy Widows
and Bric-a-Brac Sales

It was at one of the defense attorneys' seminars in the late 1950s that I first met Harvey St. Jean, criminal defense attorney from Miami. I continued to bump into Harvey from time to time at other meetings and developed a friendship of sorts with him. An ex-cop with an athlete's build and a craggy face accentuated by dark, busy eyebrows, Harvey took several years to work his way through law school. Now a well-known criminal defense attorney in and around Florida, he was at Northwestern to learn all he could about the various forensic science disciplines in order to better serve his clients.

According to one of Harvey's friends who had seen him in court, he was sort of an Andy Griffith type of defense attorney, intermittently smiling and scowling at the witness but always ready to spring the trap at the appropriate moment. His skills as a trial lawyer and his knowledge of the forensic sciences had gained him quite a reputation among the notorious, famous, or wealthy—the individuals most likely to get themselves into trouble and to be able to pay a substantial fee to have Harvey get them out of it. In a candid moment during coffee break at one of the seminars, St. Jean told me he had to charge big fees because he worked only part of the year. When he reached a certain income figure, judged by his liability to the IRS (he despised them), he would quit the practice of law entirely and retreat to some vacation resort where he hobnobbed with the local gentry or with friends of some of the defendants he had represented.

In the fall of 1960 during Harvey's "working" time of the year, he asked me to fly down to Miami to examine some documents involving wealthy 72-year-old Genevra McAlister and the "Crying Adjmis" of Miami Beach. The Adjmis were Harvey's clients, and they allegedly ran off with most of Genevra's million-and one-half dollar estate.

During the 1950s and 1960s, Lincoln Road in Miami Beach was one of the most extravagant tourist traps in the world. Prominent among the stores designed to tempt the glassy-eyed tourist were the bric-a-brac and linen shops scattered along the length of the street. Here, alluring signs advertised "imported" linen, hand carved ivory, jade, pearls from Japan, diamonds from South Africa, and even stuffed baby alligators from Columbia—always at "bargain" prices.

Two of the most lavish of these stores, or "galleries" as the owners preferred to call them, were the St. Regis and Dresden, owned and operated by Leon Adjmi and his two sons Joseph and Charles. From a modest little import rug store started by Leon when he first immigrated from Armenia, the enterprise had grown into a multi-million-dollar operation. Leon apparently owned the business, but as his two sons, Joseph and Charles, came of age, they took over its active management. More interested in money than in perpetuating whatever was left of their father's reputation, the word got around to other merchants on Lincoln Road that the Adjmi boys were pulling some shady deals. When told of this, the boys just laughed and told the others to mind their own business.

Like a fly drifting into a spider web, 72-year-old Genevra McAlister, wealthy widow of a Pittsburgh Cadillac dealer, walked into the St. Regis Gallery seeking information about the value of quartz stones she had purchased from an Atlantic City art dealer. Some months later when her relationship with the Adjmi brothers soured, she was not only less wealthy—to the tune of over one million dollars—but she was very, very *mad*—mad enough to tell her story to crime investigators for the State of Florida.

The tale she told was incredible. After becoming acquainted with the Adjmi brothers, they started to bring art objects over to her house for "storage" purposes. Included was a colorful porcelain piece of "The Last Supper" going for the price of $6,500. (This cheap Italian piece was later appraised at $250.) At the same time, McAlister's name was appearing on checks for $70,000, $90,000, and $100,000, all made payable to the Adjmis for purposes not stated on the checks. Mrs. McAlister didn't know whether or not she had signed the checks, although she did remember giving the Adjmis money to help them out of financial difficulties. Allegedly "priceless" pieces of art and jewelry were put up for collateral. On more than one occasion, said McAlister, Charles Adjmi would fall on his belly and crawl to her feet sobbing uncontrollably. They would lose the business, he cried, unless she helped them out. She would usually cave in with check payments of various amounts. When the going got particularly rough, Joseph would join in with his own peculiar brand of histrionics, which later prompted the press to label the brothers as "The Crying Adjmis."

At the same time, two salesmen for the Adjmi operation, Albert George and Emil Halfon, were concocting other schemes.

Dressed in authentic clerical garb, Albert George was introduced to Genevra as Father Leon, a Catholic priest with connections in France. According to Father Leon, a financially troubled lace factory that was the sole support of an orphanage in France was about to close its doors and desperately needed her help to survive. Determined not to let those poor children starve, Genevra paid out to the Adjmi brothers, as intermediaries in the transaction, over $600,000 for a one-third partnership in the company. The lace factory later proved to be non-existent, but the unsuspecting Genevra McAlister never knew about it until it was too late. Meanwhile, Father Leon told her about the novenas the children were saying as an expression of their gratitude. He, too, expressed his thanks by hanging a religious medal around her neck, saying, "Bless you, my child."

The second salesman for the Adjmis, Emil Halfon, set out on an even more audacious course of action. Introduced to Genevra as "Mr. John McGurney," a rich Las Vegas gambler, he proceeded to wine, dine, and flatter Mrs. McAlister in the hope that he could, perhaps, convince her to marry him. In this way he hoped to gain access to *all* of her holdings. To his pleasant surprise, during an evening characterized by more wining than dining, Genevra accepted his marriage proposal. In February of 1959, with Joseph Adjmi as witness, Mrs. Genevra McAlister became Mrs. John McGurney. A warranty deed soon followed naming the groom co-owner of her residence.

But the marriage was destined to be of short duration. Genevra began to find out some disturbing things about her new husband. His name was really Emil Halfon, he was a Muslim and not a Christian, and he was working as a salesman for Joseph and Charles Adjmi. Now, for the first time, Genevra realized that she had been hoaxed by a clever gang of con men. She was angry and ashamed all at the same time and anxious for retribution.

The Florida State's Attorney's office immediately filed charges of grand larceny against the Adjmi brothers and their father, together with Emil Halfon and Albert George. Following a grand jury hearing, all five were indicted, and the case was sent down for trial before Criminal Court Judge George Schulz and a six-man jury.

As defense attorney for the Crying Adjmis gang, Harvey St. Jean faced one of the toughest challenges of his professional career. Realizing that all of the machinations of his clients were bound to come out at the trial, St. Jean adopted a "Let the buyer beware" defense to the allegations of Genevra McAlister. Wasn't she a sophisticated woman who invested in the stock market and managed her own business affairs including her husband's estate?

Her own attorneys would testify to the fact that she never signed anything without reading it over carefully. And she knew that some of the deals the Adjmis offered her were too good to be true, but in her greed to make a lot of money she went along with them. "Let the buyer beware" warnings were there from the first moment she purchased art work from the Adjmis to the time she married the phony John McGurney, but she didn't heed them.

Harvey St. Jean had one more ace in the hole. His questioned document expert, Donald Doud, had examined the signatures on scores of checks, contracts, stock documents, and a warranty deed and had found them all to be genuinely signed by Mrs. McAlister. I sat in the courtroom during St. Jean's cross-examination of Genevra McAlister and could sense the frustration he obviously felt at her answers. A pleasant-looking woman of medium build with dyed dark hair and a younger appearance than her seventy-two years, Genevra answered all questions in a calm, but mostly ambiguous, manner. (Rumor had it that she didn't want to disturb a $300,000 settlement agreement reached with the Adjmis.)

When asked about the checks made payable to Joseph and Charles Adjmis, she couldn't remember whether or not she had signed them, although the signatures did look like hers. Neither could Genevra remember why she would ever make out checks to the Adjmis for such large sums of money. "There were too many of them," she said. When pressed on the subject, Genevra stated, "All I know is they cleaned me." Questioned about other documents such as contracts for purchase of antiques and art, the warranty deed executed during her marriage to "John McGurney," and some stock documents, she couldn't remember whether or not she had signed them. If the signatures were indeed genuine, Joseph Adjmi might have hypnotized her into signing the blank documents, the upper part of which they later filled in.

Harvey St. Jean had introduced me to the Adjmi brothers at one of the court recesses. It was true, both were extremely charismatic individuals. Joseph, at twenty-four, was a handsome, swarthy type with a full head of wavy hair. But the most compelling part of Joseph's appearance was his eyes, which were framed by a pair of dark-rimmed spectacles, the center portions of which were highly magnified, giving his eyes a peculiar penetrating quality. At one recess following Mrs. McAlister's testimony, Joseph came out of the courtroom chuckling to himself and addressed one of the co-defendants sitting beside me on the bench. "Did you hear what Genevra just said? She said that I had hypnotic eyes and made her do things against her will by power of suggestion. If that's true, I have missed my calling!" But hypnotic eyes or not, it was easy to understand how Joseph Adjmi, in his expensive, made-to-order suits and attentive, suave manner, completely captivated the vulnerable Genevra McAlister.

Charles Adjmi, two years older than his brother, was also good looking, curly haired, and charismatic, but in a different way. His limpid eyes and baby-face expression lent themselves well to the sobbing, sometimes hysterical performances he put on for Genevra's benefit. He didn't have the brains of his brother, but he had an acting ability that served them well. For obvious reasons, neither of the brothers was put on the witness stand by St. Jean, nor were co-defendants Albert George and Emil Halfon. The only one who testified was Leon Adjmi, the boys' father.

When Harvey St. Jean called me as a witness, I used a number of enlarged comparison exhibits to illustrate the reasons for my opinion that Mrs. McAlister genuinely signed all of the questioned documents. She wrote a highly developed, skillful signature, I told the jury, and I could find no evidence whatsoever of forgery. Everything about the signatures proclaimed genuineness! As to her claim that she may have signed documents in blank, I did find one contract where that probably happened. Using an accurately ruled typewriting test plate, it was clear that the underscore line beneath the signature was out of alignment with the typing in the body of the document. But whether McAlister was "hypnotized" into signing a blank document, only the Adjmi boys could say—and they were not talking.

At the conclusion of my direct examination, the prosecutor cross-examined me only briefly. There was really no reason to do more. I had simply confirmed, in somewhat less ambiguous terms, Mrs. McAlister's previous testimony.

With the case completed and now in the hands of the jury, Harvey St. Jean's "Let the buyer beware" defense strategy seemed to have been a pretty good one. The prosecution, in effect, conceded that Mrs. McAlister genuinely signed all of the documents in question, as I had testified. And, if she knew she was being hypnotized into signing blank documents or unduly influenced by the Adjmis' crying act, why did she continue to pay out money to them? The admonition, "Let the buyer beware" should have been ringing in her ears.

But the jury didn't quite buy Harvey's argument. It took them only two hours to come back with a verdict. Joseph and Charles Adjmi, Emil Halfon, and Albert George were all found guilty of grand larceny and were given the maximum sentences of five years each. The boys' father, Leon Adjmi, was acquitted.

But that was not the end of the story. While released on $25,000 bail each, pending results of appeals to the Florida Supreme Court, Charles, Joseph and their father Leon Adjmi were re-indicted in an entirely different case involving charges of insurance fraud. It would appear that five bric-a-brac galleries on Lincoln Road, including one owned by the Adjmis, mysteriously caught fire and sustained substantial damage. If found guilty of starting any of the fires, the Adjmis could go to prison for as long as thirty years each.

Whether Harvey St. Jean represented the Adjmis in this new legal scrape I cannot say. I lost touch with him after the McAlister case, and unfortunately he is not around today to tell us about it. In *The Corpse Had a Familiar Face*,[1] Miami wrtter Edna Buchanan describes a murder scene where a body is slumped over the steering

---

1. Edna Buchanan, *The Corpse Had a Familiar Face: Covering Miami, America's Hottest Beat* (New York: Random House, 1987).

wheel of a parked, lime-green Cadillac Coupe de Ville.

"I leaned over carefully, without touching the car, and peered inside," reported Buchanan. "The corpse had a familiar face. To the thatch of silver gray hair, the ferociously dark and shaggy eyebrows, something had been added: powder burns. They smudged the flesh around the two holes in his left temple. An exit wound on the right side of his face had bloodied his cheek. 'It is your friend and mine, Mr. St. Jean,' the detective said. 'Harvey St. Jean apparently made some enemies along the way.' They never found out who did it."

Buchanan's book makes no mention of the Adjmis and whether or not one of them was suspected of pulling the trigger. I personally doubt that they had anything to do with Harvey's demise. They were more into crying than killing.

A Forgery Experiment
with a Surprising Outcome

Upon returning to Chicago following the Adjmi case, I called my friend Fred Inbau at Northwestern University Law School to verify plans for my next appearance before his scientific evidence class. I could sense the excitement in Fred's voice as he told about a new handwriting experiment he had cooked up to illustrate the topic of one of my lectures, "Signature Forgeries." In a carefully controlled experiment, he would ask each student to forge the signature of a colleague and then submit the results for class analysis. I was enthusiastic about Fred's idea, which I felt would set to rest a question I was always asked by skeptics in my classes: "Mr. Doud, is there such a thing as a perfect forger that you or no other expert could detect?"

Knowing that a yes, no, or don't know answer would simply provoke more questions, I usually fell back on the old cliche: "If a forgery was that perfectly executed and absent any of the telltale signs of attempted imitation, I would, of course, be unable to detect it." Judging by the knowing glances exchanged between some of the students, this was not a satisfying answer at all. They demanded absolute, positive, overwhelming proof of everything I said. As a professor experienced in the ways of law students, Fred Inbau knew how to provide that proof.

As it turned out, about thirty students of Fred's Scientific Evidence classes participated in our signature forgery experiment. Realizing that students sometimes love to play games with guest lecturers and professors, Inbau and I took great pains to avoid any possible "fool the expert" type of scheme. We did this by handing the students sheets of ruled paper with each line numbered and instructions to place one signature in a special area at the top of the sheet as the control or "exemplar" specimen. They were then to place four to six additional signatures on the numbered lines below, skipping certain lines in a random fashion and otherwise trying to avoid any definite pattern of signature placement. A separate record was to be kept of the lines on which the genuine signatures were placed.

The first part of the experiment went off without a hitch, and Inbau now transferred the sheets bearing the genuine signatures to students on the far side of the room. He also transferred the pen originally used because different colored inks would have been a dead giveaway. The students then took up the task of trying to imitate the signatures on the sheet assigned to them. As I looked around the room, I could see some very pained expressions as they realized how difficult this seemingly simple task was.

At the conclusion of the fifteen-minute time limit, I set up my opaque projector and confidently proceeded to point out to my young audience the fatal flaws I had found in each forgery attempt—the excessive tremor, the letter form differences, the blunt beginning and ending strokes, the unusual pen lifts and joins. Then the unthinkable happened. Towards the end of the stack, I ran across one sheet that literally jerked me out of my complacency. All of the signatures on that page looked alike! I pulled the sheet from the projector and, using a low power magnifier, looked and compared and looked again. I simply could not tell which signatures were forged and which were genuine. All of the students in the room roared with laughter at my discomfort.

Feeling that Inbau and I had somehow or other been duped despite our careful efforts to avoid collusion of any kind, I took the offending sheet of signatures back to my laboratory, intent upon salvaging what was left of my reputation. There, using an eight-power stereo-zoom microscope, I discovered in the genuine signatures the minute hooks, and almost imperceptible pen lifts and pressure points that separated them from the "forgeries." When I reported the results of my examination back to the class, they passed me with a 100 score.

The student who possessed this amazing ability to rapidly and skillfully imitate signatures turned out to be a good looking young man who was not even aware of his unique talent. When I told him that he ranked alongside a handful of other expert forgers whose work I had seen, he commented: "Mr. Doud, you don't have to worry about me. I am studying to be a prosecutor. I expect to be tough on criminals."

I thought of that young man a few years later during my examination of the Clifford Irving-Howard Hughes autobiography documents—I thought of him a lot!

5

The Howard Hughes - Clifford Irving Autobiography Hoax

Is not this a lamentable thing, that the skin of an innocent lamb should be made into parchment? That parchment, being scribbled o'er, should undo a man?

WILLIAM SHAKESPEARE, Henry VI

The Prince of Thieves Almost Succeeds

In underworld idiom, the forger is known as the "Prince of Thieves," obviously referring to the audacious, non-violent, and frequently elegant nature of this type of criminal. Clifford Irving, the architect of the Howard Hughes autobiography hoax, fit this description perfectly and, in some respects, elevated his role to an even more lofty status. For Irving became adept not only in forging

Hughes's handwriting but also in emulating Hughes's thinking process and unique, sometimes profane, style of expressing himself. Like Pygmalion, Clifford Irving was somehow or other able to turn himself into a remarkably close copy of Howard Hughes. Indeed, the transformation was so successful that he was able to deceive a sophisticated editorial staff of McGraw-Hill Publishing Company and *Life* magazine, a number of members of the press, plus two firms of questioned document examiners.

Was I fooled by Clifford Irving's forgeries? You will have to read the rest of this chapter to find out. But I will give you a clue. It was what I discovered under the microscope that led me irresistibly to a final conclusion.

O'Hare Field in Chicago was the ideal setting for a meeting to discuss Howard Hughes's alleged autobiography. Many of the planes that rattled the windows of the executive suite where McGraw-Hill attorney Harold Altman and I met that cold, snowy afternoon of January 11, 1972, were part of Hughes's former TWA empire, and virtually all of them contained innovations pioneered by Hughes himself or by the Hughes Aircraft Company. Hughes had landed on occasion at O'Hare Field and in his younger days would have felt right at home in the cockpit of one of these giant aircraft.

Earlier that morning I had received an urgent call from Altman in New York requesting that I meet him at O'Hare that afternoon to discuss the Hughes autobiography and, more specifically, several letters authorizing author Clifford Irving to write it. They wanted to be sure the documents were authentic. On January 18th, a week hence, *Life* magazine was to announce plans for releasing a three part, serialized version of the autobiography, and time was of the essence. McGraw-Hill planned to later publish the autobiography in book form.

On the drive down to O'Hare Field, I mentally reviewed some of the things I had read in the press about this astonishing, stranger-than-fiction drama and the people involved in it.

Clifford Irving was leading man and, as I was later to learn, the undisputed "Prince of Thieves." A tall, elegant, dark-haired man in his early forties, Irving was the epitome of the gentleman of letters. With his fourth wife Edith and two children, he lived on the tiny island of Ibiza, off the coast of Spain. One writer referred to those who resided in Ibiza as "that Lost Legion of expatriate pseudo-intellectual jet-set poseurs," a characterization that only partially described Irving. He possessed a great deal more imagination and creative energy than most of his fellow Ibizans, having authored a half-dozen books of fiction and non-fiction. With possibly one or two exceptions, none, however, proved to be financially successful. McGraw-Hill published two of these and in the process, set the stage for its future role as Irving's unwitting ally in the Hughes autobiography fiasco.

Irving's last and most ambitious writing effort, until the Hughes autobiography, was a book called *Fake![1]* about Elmyr de Hory, described on the flyleaf as "the world's greatest art forger." This, too, had disappointing sales, although it received considerable attention at the time of the Hughes autobiography affair because of the forgery issue and de Hory's reputed skill at forging paintings and the signatures on them.

The reluctant co-star of this drama was Howard Hughes, reclusive billionaire and mystery man. Although he never appeared in person during the entire course of the autobiography dispute, a group of reporters listened to a voice from the Bahamas over transatlantic cable that claimed to be his. A personal appearance was hardly necessary anyway. Hughes's reputation spoke just as eloquently about his strange, iconoclastic habits. A genius of a man who pioneered the manufacture and design of aircraft, owned and ran TWA Airlines for a time, purchased RKO Studios and established himself as an important figure in the movie-making industry, Hughes became one of the real celebrities of his time. For reasons about which one can only speculate, Hughes in his later years became a reclusive eccentric whose obsessive need for privacy became so all-consuming that he literally withdrew from life. A skeleton of a man demanding daily administrations of codeine and Valium by his "palace guard" aides, Hughes saved his urine in bottles and spent virtually all of his time watching old

---

1. Clifford Irving, *Fake! The Story of Elmyr de Hory, the Greatest Art Forger of Our Time* (New York: McGraw-Hill, Inc. 1969).

movies from his earlier RKO days. "Outlaw," "Scarface," and "Bullet for a Badman" were but a few of the films he watched over and over again on a twelve-hour basis.

A fugitive from numerous lawsuits, Hughes fled Las Vegas in 1970 for a more peaceful existence in other parts of the world including the Bahamas, Nicaragua, Canada, and Mexico. Within two years, his peace was again to be shattered by allegations surrounding the preparation of an astonishing document purporting to be the story of his own life.

The genesis of the Hughes autobiography affair came about on January 3, 1971, when Clifford Irving wrote a letter of most intriguing content to Beverly Loo, Executive Editor of McGraw-Hill Publishing Company, with whom he had become acquainted during the publication of *Fake!* It read:

> I sent a copy of *Fake!* some time ago to Howard Hughes, and to my surprise received a note of thanks and praise from him. Some wheels are beginning to turn in my brain. Do you know if there is any biography of Hughes or anything in the works for the near future? Let me know, but please don't mention it to anyone.

The "note of thanks and praise" from Hughes, to which Irving referred was, in fact, a two-page letter handwritten on yellow legal size paper that read

Dear Mr. Irving:

Thank you for the gift of your book (*Fake!*), which I thoroughly enjoyed reading. Your inscription was very thoughtful.

I find myself deeply interested in the fellow you have written about despite a natural inclination to the contrary. I cannot help wondering what has happened to him.

I would hate to think what other biographers might have done to him, but it seems to me that you have portrayed your man with great consideration and sympathy, when it would have been tempting to do otherwise. For reasons you may readily understand, this has impressed me.

I do remember your father and I was sorry to learn of his passing.

Yours truly,
H. R. Hughes

As can be imagined, Beverly Loo and the other McGraw-Hill editors were ecstatic at the thought of publishing an authorized Howard Hughes biography. The New York literary world had been salivating for twenty years over the increasingly faint prospect that such an event would occur. Now Clifford Irving had offered new hope in the form of a tantalizing letter from Howard Hughes himself. Irving must have been secretly pleased at the enthusiastic response with which his information was received by McGraw-

Hill. "Pursue the matter with all of your energy," said editor Beverly Loo, "and let me know immediately if and when you again hear from Hughes." They didn't have long to wait.

On January 30, Irving again wrote McGraw-Hill from Ibiza and reported receiving two additional handwritten letters from Hughes, the second of which was especially exciting. "This letter," Irving gleefully wrote editor Beverly Loo, "virtually commits Howard Hughes to the biographical project I suggested to him."

The euphoria at McGraw Hill was indescribable. "Come to New York immediately," said Beverly Loo in a long distance call to Ibiza, "and we will work out terms of a contract proposal you can offer to Howard Hughes." Her optimism over the financial aspects of the deal might have been somewhat diminished had she known what tough bargainers Clifford Irving and the invisible Howard Hughes would be.

Upon arriving in New York, Irving immediately taxied to the McGraw-Hill offices where he showed to Beverly Loo and the others on the editorial staff the three letters he had received from Howard Hughes. The last one, written in a bold, flowing hand, was exactly as described by Irving in his letter to Beverly Loo. It read:

> Dear Mr. Irving:
>
> I thank you again for the pleasantness of your letter to me. I am not "horrified" by your suggestion, although in times past it has come to me from other quarters and was rejected by me. You must know that

a short time ago a man named Gerber[1] published a book which purported to be the story of my life. I found it in part offensive and in part childish.

I am not entirely insensitive to what journalists have written about me and for that reason I have the deepest respect for your treatment of de Hory, however much I may disapprove of his morals. I do not question your integrity and I would not expect you to question mine.

It would not suit me to die without having certain misconceptions cleared up and without having stated the truth about my life. The immorality you speak of does not interest me, not in this world. I believe in obligations. I regret many things in the past, but I have little feelings of shame about them.

I would be grateful if you would let me know when and how you would wish to undertake the writing of the biography you proposed.

I wish there to be no publicity about this communication for the time being, and I would view a breach of this request very unfavorably.

Sincerely yours,
H. R. Hughes

---

1. Albert Gerber, *Bashful Billionaire: An Unauthorized Biography of Howard Hughes* (New York: Lyle Stuart, Inc., New York, 1967).

When one of the McGraw-Hill editors suggested the possibility that this letter might be a forgery, Beverly Loo recalled seeing a genuine sample of Hughes's writing in the January 22, 1971, edition of *Life*, and commented that to her it looked identical to the writing on the three Irving letters.

When Beverly Loo broached the subject of finances, Irving told her that, before coming to New York, he had contacted Howard Hughes to see whether he still wanted to go ahead with the project and on what financial basis. Hughes told him, yes, he was anxious to get started as soon as possible but felt a contract should first be drawn up that would cover all possible contingencies. Would Clifford Irving be able to meet with him in Oaxaca, Mexico, to discuss the details? Of course Irving would.

In the end it took a second "meeting" between Irving and Hughes, this time supposedly in San Juan, Puerto Rico, and several, sometimes heated, sessions between Irving and McGraw-Hill editors, before a contract was finally drawn up. It agreed to pay "H. R. Hughes" a total of $750,000 in installments and Irving himself about half of that amount. The last payments were to be made following completion and delivery of the final autobiography manuscript.

With the pecuniary interests out of the way, Irving then told McGraw-Hill that he would be devoting the next several months to taping interviews with Howard Hughes. When completed, Irving said, the tapes would be transcribed and edited into the question and answer format of the interviews themselves.

For almost five months from early May to September 13, 1971, Clifford Irving's only contact with McGraw-Hill was through cables and telephone calls, some of which originated in Mexico, the Bahamas, and other places where he was supposed to be interviewing Howard Hughes. If this jumping from one place to another by Howard Hughes seemed incongruous to anyone at McGraw-Hill, it wasn't sufficiently disturbing to hire an investigator to check airline, hotel, or other sources of information. Had they done so, they would have found the object of some of Irving's "interviews" to be a svelte Danish singer and actress, the Baroness Nina Van Pallandt. "How could Cliffy be interviewing Howard Hughes when he never left my side for one moment?" she later cooed to one reporter.

Finally, in September of 1971, McGraw-Hill's suspicions regarding the legitimacy of Irving's autobiography project were put to rest. Luxuriating in princely splendor at the New York Elysee Hotel, Irving called Beverly Loo to invite her and two Time-Life editors to a preview showing of Howard Hughes's own autobiography—at least the transcribed version of it. As the three editors entered Irving's suite, he ceremoniously handed Beverly Loo a foot-high stack of documents purportedly representing transcriptions of countless taped interviews with Howard Hughes. It was reported that the editors were so anxious to view the contents of the manuscript that they literally tore it apart so that each one could read a section at a time. Clifford Irving, who paced the floor restlessly awaiting the final verdict, must have been exceedingly pleased and relieved to overhear chuckles, whoops, and hollers from the trio, reacting to some of the scandalous, outrageous, and candid comments made by Hughes. The language appeared to be vintage Howard Hughes. Ralph Graves, Executive Editor of *Life*, put it this way:

> It was outspoken, full of rich and outrageous anecdotes, as well as detailed accounts of Hughes's youth, his movie making, his career in aviation, his business affairs, his private life, his opinions and crotchets. He explained why he phoned people on business matters in the middle of the night (he kept strange hours anyway and it caught them at their weakest moment). He explained his philosophy of business negotiation (one man plays the lion, one man plays the donkey). He told business yarns ranging from high finance in TWA to the time a high-ranking corporate friend was caught swiping a box of cookies from the supermarket. Even the boring parts were persuasive: Howard Hughes had always been fascinated by the minutiae of aircraft design and performance, and the transcript had lots of it.

The preface to the Hughes autobiography, allegedly dictated to Clifford Irving by Howard Hughes, sounded equally authentic. As a smashing introduction to the autobiography, it simply couldn't be beat:

PREFACE

It was never my intention to cut along the dotted line and write a standard, polite autobiography. I believe that more lies have been printed and told about me than about any living man – therefore it is my purpose in this book to restore the balance and set the record straight forever. Several biographies of me have been published before – all of them misleading and childish. I am certain that in the future more lies and rubbish will appear. I chose to work with Clifford Irving because of his sympathy, his discernment and discretion; and, as I learned, his integrity as a human being. The story of our meetings and how my life was swallowed up and spat back at me by a tape recorder, I leave to him. I should make it clear that I do not agree with everything he has to say, either in his introduction to this book or in his notes; but I do not dispute his right to say it.

The end result of our work together was not the biography that either of us had originally planned. The book you hold in your hands is my own narrative of my life. The words – other than some of the questions which provoked them – are my own spoken words. The thoughts, opinions and recollections, the descriptions of events and personalities, are my own. I have not permitted them to be emasculated or polished because I decided, after the many interviews had been completed, that this was as close as I could get to the elusive, often painful truth. Let it stand.

I believe you will realize that I have tried very hard to tell the truth. I have lived a full life and, perhaps, what may seem a strange life – even to myself. I refuse to apologize, although I am willing now to explain as best I can. I regret much of the past, but I have little feelings of shame about it. I did, as I will relate, what I believed I had to do in order to come out whole.

Call this my autobiography. Call it my memoirs – call it what you please. It is the story of my life in my own words.

/s/ Howard Hughes

With the Hughes autobiography manuscript in hand, McGraw-Hill and Time-Life interests lost no time in arranging for publication of the serialized accounts and the book that one editor predicted would "outsell the *Bible*." Only one other precaution was necessary—to set to rest any lingering doubts, especially those in the minds of Hughes Tool Company attorneys, that the letters from Hughes, which had now grown to a total of five, plus the contract and check signatures, might not be in the handwriting of Howard Hughes. Two different firms of questioned document examiners were consulted to make that determination. Apparently working from high-contrast photographs of the autobiography writings and the known Hughes specimens, both firms pronounced the autobiography documents to be genuine.

Now certain "unsettling events" were beginning to take place almost on a daily basis. For example, Hughes Tool Company attorneys threatened to bring suit against McGraw-Hill if they proceeded with plans to publish the alleged autobiography. Equally serious, Hughes interests were threatening to obtain a court injunction barring *Life* from printing the first serialized version of it. And even the unflappable Clifford Irving began to squirm and perspire under questioning about seeming inconsistencies in his story. When asked to produce the tapes of his interviews with Hughes, Irving stated, "Naturally, I returned them all to Hughes."

It was quite apparent that McGraw-Hill and Time-Life now found themselves in a catch twenty-two position, with Clifford Irving's persuasive evidence and the opinions of two handwriting firms supporting their contention that the letters and other documents were written by Hughes, and other recent developments, including Hughes's alleged voice from the Bahamas denying that he knew anything about an autobiography, raising some troubling questions. *Life* magazine, the holder of the serial rights to the autobiography, was champing at the bit because of publication deadlines. No wonder McGraw-Hill was anxious to get another expert opinion on the handwriting issue—*fast*. My name was chosen to conduct the examination, I was told, because of my experience and reputation in the field and the location of my practice in the Midwest.

The table in the O'Hare Field executive suite was too small to accommodate all of the document photographs disgorged from attorney Alan Altman's briefcase, and I can remember feeling a little foolish and unprofessional as the two of us squatted down on the floor to view the thirty or more 11 x 14 photographs Altman spread out before us. An intense, middle-aged powerhouse of a man, Altman seemed oblivious to the amused stares of others in the room as we crawled from document to document to better view each photograph. I hunched down inside my coat, hoping that I would not be seen by anyone I knew.

The unusual circumstances surrounding my first view of the questioned documents were soon forgotten as I concentrated on the evidence spread out on the floor before me—evidence upon which I hoped to base a scientific conclusion. My first concern was about the quality of the photographic copies, which were made with a high contrast photographic material that produced very little detail in the strokes of the handwriting. On the other hand, there was an extraordinary amount of evidence–the autobiography writings (five signed letters totaling fourteen pages in all, plus six other signatures on an agreement), the McGraw-Hill contract, the preface to the autobiography, and endorsements of McGraw-Hill's checks payable to H. R. Hughes.. I can remember thinking to myself that there is no forger alive with a mind retentive enough to memorize all of the nuances of Howard Hughes's writing and the hand skill to incorporate them into extending writings of this magnitude. But I was jumping to conclusions. Clifford Irving was not your average forger and, as events were later to show, knew exactly what to do and what to avoid in his efforts to achieve his final goal.

I next turned to the stack of photographs representing Howard Hughes's known handwriting. Unfortunately, the quality of the photographs proved to be little better than the autobiography material, with critical detail being missing from the writings. To compound the problem, most of Hughes's genuine signatures were signed to documents dated in the late 1930s, towards the beginning of World War II. The signatures on the autobiography documents were allegedly written thirty years later, a wide time gap to bridge in comparing handwriting.

Approaching the bottom of the pile, my spirits were suddenly lifted when I found several signed Nevada Gaming Commission documents dated during the same 1971 period as the five questioned letters. I also came across a three-page letter in Hughes's handwriting dated 12-10-70 addressed to "Dear Chester and Bill." "Chester" was Chester Davis, legal counsel for Hughes, and "Bill" was Bill Gay, vice president of Hughes Tool Company. By virtue of this outspoken and explicit letter from Hughes, the two men were directed to fire Robert Maheu, chief of Hughes's Nevada operations. The three pages of cursive script written by Hughes represented a bonanza in upper and lower case letters, as did the bold signature, "Howard R. Hughes" at the end. I would need this writing and every one of the other exemplars to unravel the mystery of the alleged Howard Hughes autobiography. When asked about the availability of the original documents, Altman indicated that he could not run the risk of bringing them to Chicago, but if I needed to examine them at some future time I could do so at

McGraw-Hill's New York office.

As Altman packed up for his return trip to New York, he turned to me and remarked almost as an afterthought, "By the way, Mr. Doud, you might be interested in knowing that portions of the "Chester and Bill" letter, including Hughes's signature, were reproduced in *Newsweek* magazine for December 21, 1970, and in the January 22, 1971, edition of *Life*. You can probably get copies at some used bookstore." Altman may not have known it at the time, but his last-minute revelation was to open my eyes to an entirely new line of inquiry.

The day after my conference with Altman, I was in my laboratory early, eager to start the adventure of comparing Howard Hughes's known writing with the writings on the autobiography documents. When I say "adventure," I have always looked upon the process of comparing handwriting in suspected forgery cases as an exciting quest into the unknown where my skills as a questioned document examiner are pitted against those of the forger. More often than not, that individual turns out to be an incompetent amateur whose bungled attempt at imitation contains all the classic evidences of forgery including what document examiners refer to as "the tremor of fraud." But watch out! When you least expect it, a skilled forger comes along, and he can challenge your ability to the limit. What starts off as an "adventure" can turn into a nightmare.

The evidence I search for in trying to determine whether a writing is genuine or forged is in some ways comparable to the clues the criminalist looks for in trying to track down a suspect from tool mark impressions, bullets, hair, or DNA traces left at the crime scene.

Clues? There are literally scores of them in the handwriting of most people. They tell the experienced observer something about the writing system that person was taught, whether he or she learned to write in some foreign country, of the writer's skill and fluency in executing the letter forms, of the pressure exerted on the writing instrument, of the variation range in the writing, or serious illnesses that may have affected the ability of the muscles and nerves to control the pen, and finally of each mature person's personalized habits of forming the upper and lower case letters. Included in the wonderfully unique writing habits of individuals, and especially those who write frequently, are the delicate hooks, pen lifts, retraced lines, and pressure points that can best be observed microscopically. They are also the features that a forger most often fails to observe and, therefore, does not incorporate into his forgery. Poorly made photographs may obscure part or all of this important evidence.

My plan for examining the autobiography documents was to first take up the signature aspect of the problem and then, later, the fourteen pages of cursive writings. After all, it was the Howard Hughes signatures that provided the legal basis for Clifford Irving's claims, and this seemed like the logical way to proceed. But logical or not, the signatures were far from the best way of introducing me to the machinations of Clifford Irving, especially when the evidence consisted of high contrast photographs. I spent an inordinate amount of time considering and reconsidering all aspects of the signature evidence, but in the end I was glad that I did. It gave me a preview of the pitfalls that lay ahead when I finally got around to examining the cursive writings, all fourteen pages of them.

My method of examining signature problems, especially when the originals were not available, was to prepare composite study charts, facilitating a close comparison of the signatures for variation range, size, slant, letter forms, and similar handwriting features. When I juxtaposed the nine Hughes exemplars with the eleven autobiography signatures, my initial reaction was that they had all been written by the same person, namely Howard Hughes. There were many striking similarities between the two sets of writings. Then I took a closer look. Considering the wide variation range in Hughes's own signature, there seemed to be slight differences in his usual habits of beginning the *H*, the manner in which the baseline of the *w* descended, the bent back of the *h* ,and the direction and short ending to the *s*. Seeds of suspicion had now been sown, and I began to seriously entertain the thought that I might be dealing with the work of an expert forger.

In a letter to Alan Altman written the day after my initial examination, I stated, "Certainly it cannot be denied that, if the questioned writings are not genuine, they are highly skilled imitations of some known specimens of Howard Hughes's signature."

And what would be the most available source of Hughes's genuine signatures? It was at that point that the implication of Altman's statement regarding the *Newsweek and Life* reproductions of the "Chester and Bill" letter finally struck home. Judging by the difficulty McGraw-Hill had in securing original specimens of Hughes's writing for my examination, a potential forger would likely find it even more difficult and turn to some published source of that writing. Hadn't Altman told me that the *Newsweek* and *Life* reproductions of the "Chester and Bill" letter were the only printed versions of Hughes's writing available? If all that seemed simple, it wasn't. Searching for a possible connection between the eleven autobiography signatures and a single reproduced example of Hughes's signature would require some very creative efforts. But at least I knew where to begin.

I immediately went to the Renaissance Book Shop (a used book store in Milwaukee) and purchased copies of *Newsweek* and *Life* magazine for the desired dates. The short *Newsweek* reproduction was reduced in size and appeared to be an unlikely source for any forgery. *Life* magazine, on the other hand, displayed a crisp, clear, two-page spread of almost the entire document, at the end of which was a bold signature, "Howard R. Hughes."

I searched my reference files for any technical papers on the subject of connecting several forged signatures to a single known specimen other than by evidence of tracing, which was not a factor here. I could find nothing written on the subject and decided instead to follow my own instincts. The answer was not long in coming, but it seemed designed more to confuse than to enlighten. Of the six autobiography signatures where the name "Howard" was used, every one contained a definite pen lift between the *o* and *w* of Howard. The *o* and *w* in the *Life* example were connected, thereby exploding any theory that one was copied from the other. And that wasn't all. Three of the autobiography signatures were written "Howard Hughes" without the *R* in the *Life* example, and five others abbreviated to "H. R. Hughes".

My notes of this examination stated: "Cannot definitely connect questioned signatures to *Life* exemplar. Difference in connecting stroke between *o* and *w*."

It was now January 15th, four days after my initial conference with Alan Altman. I had been delayed in completing my examination of the Irving-Hughes autobiography documents by an Appleton case requiring trial preparation, and I was beginning to worry about finishing the project before the January 18th deadline. I could foresee spending a few evening hours in my laboratory trying to get a handle on this inherently difficult case, made more difficult by the high contrast photographs presented for examination. If the cursive writings proved to be as perplexing as the signatures, my wife Jane and son Bob would be having dinner alone for several nights.

Determining the status of the handwriting on the five questioned letters would involve the same general procedures as the signature problem—preparation of enlarged comparison charts of questioned and known writings. Because it was obviously impossible to illustrate all of the letters and words involved, certain examples would be selected that seemed to represent the norm in the writing. I have been cross-examined many times about the selection process I use in preparing my courtroom comparison exhibits, implying that I might have unfairly selected examples to conform to my opinion. I have always been able to defuse that issue by pointing out to the jury other examples that were just as close that I would have included on my chart had there been room.

But my first step was to take the photographs submitted by Altman and make a side-by-side comparison of the first Hughes letter allegedly written to Irving and page one of the "Chester and Bill" letter. I wanted to see how the writings compared in general features. As my eye passed from one document to the other, my first impression was that Howard Hughes had written the autobiography document. It looked like his writing and failed to show any of the "tremor of fraud" one would expect from a forgery.

But then as I searched for individual examples of letters and words to compare and add to my study exhibits, I began to see differences, some slight, some more pronounced and persistent. Now a definite trend seemed to be developing. The right shoulder of the y's in "you" and "your" was definitely lower in Hughes's known writing, the left portion of the w was smaller and more elevated above the baseline, the connecting stroke between the o and f was more diagonal in its direction, the crossing of the t was higher, and even the quotation marks differed in degree of curvature.

It was beginning to look like McGraw-Hill had been hoaxed by a very clever forger. But I still needed to examine the original documents in McGraw-Hill's possession to verify what I had observed and to look for hidden evidence not visible in the photographs. In particular, I would search for the microscopic retrace strokes, delicate pen lifts, tapering endings, tiny hooks, and other minutia that would be difficult, if not impossible, for a forger of Hughes's writing to see and to imitate, especially if the source of his copy was a reproduction of the "Chester and Bill" letter in *Life* magazine and not the original.

Using a reproduction of the "Chester and Bill" letter as his copying source might pose another, even more deadly, threat to the wood-be forger. He would have to limit the capitals and small letters of his forgery to exactly the same as those appearing in the *Life* reproduction. To use any other would be disastrous. The letter forms certainly wouldn't look like Hughes's and might well be similar to those of the forger's.

The only way to resolve this problem, I reluctantly decided, was to go through the tedious process of alphabetically tabulating all of the capitals and small letters used in the "Chester and Bill" reprint and then going through the same exercise with the fourteen pages of autobiography writing. Once I got started and began tabulating the results, it became increasingly less tedious as I began to see a pattern unfolding—an unusual coincidence between the two sets of documents in the capitals and small letters used. At the

Dear Chester and Bill —

I do not understand why the problem of Maheu is not yet fully settled and why this bad publicity seems to continue. It could hurt our company's valuable properties in Nevada, and also the entire state.

I believe my company is one of the biggest employers (if not the biggest) in the state, and surely what damages an entity employing this many Nevadans is bad for the state itself.)

You told me that, if I called Governor Laxalt and District Attorney George Franklin, it would put an end to this problem.

I made these calls, and I do not understand why this very damaging publicity should continue merely because the properly constituted board of directors of Hughes Tool Company decided, for reasons they considered just, to terminate all relationship with Maheu and Hooper.

Page 1 of "Chester and Bill" letter.

end of the day, I leaned back in my chair in both amazement and bewilderment. I had found identically the same thirteen capitals used in *both* sets of documents–the *A, B, C, D, F, G, H, I, L, M, N,* and *T*. And, of the lower case letters, all but the letter *z* coincided. Was all of this just accidental? It defied common sense to think so, yet it was also hard to believe that any forger would have the cleverness, foresight, and patience to draft fourteen pages of autobiography writings using *only* those thirteen capitals and all but one of the lower case letters.

And what about the *z*'s found only in the autobiography documents? They differed somewhat from Hughes's known writing but not enough on which to draw any definite conclusion. It was but one additional clue. The differences I had found between Hughes's known writings and the handwritings on the five autobiography letters were far more compelling.

It was January 18th, the deadline set by Altman for reporting the results of my examination. I was in Appleton, Wisconsin, where the Circuit Court judge had just declared an afternoon recess following my testimony. Impatient to get my call through to New York by 5:00 PM Eastern Time, I dashed out into the hall to find the nearest pay telephone. I am always pumped up with adrenaline when I testify in court, and now I had a double dose as my attempts to reach McGraw-Hill lawyer Alan Altman were frustrated by a bevy of telephone operators who transferred me from one department to another searching for the illusive Mr. Altman. Finally a familiar voice answered the phone.

"How are you, Mr. Doud? Got good news for us?"

I took a deep breath. "No, Mr. Altman, I'm afraid it's just the opposite. It is beginning to look like all of the documents you submitted for my examination are forged. This includes the handwriting on the five letters and the signatures on all of the other documents including the contract and check endorsements. I will, of course, want to confirm these tentative findings by examination of the original documents."

All was silent on the other end of the line. Finally, in a voice charged with emotion, Altman literally shouted into the phone. "You are entitled to your opinion, Mr. Doud, but who do you think McGraw-Hill should believe—one expert from Milwaukee or members of two prominent firms from New York?" (Did I detect a hint of Eastern snobbery in that statement?)

Stung by the unfairness of Altman's remark, I put the question right back to him. "Do you think McGraw-Hill should decide a question of this importance on the basis of a head count? I don't."

I might have been a little less impatient with Altman had I known that, earlier that same morning, three executives of the McGraw-Hill and Time-Life organizations had appeared in court to present affidavits swearing to their belief in the authenticity of the autobiography and accompanying documents. The affidavits ran exactly counter to my report that the documents were forged:

Harold McGraw (President, McGraw-Hill Publishing):

I believe the book Clifford Irving has produced is

precisely what it is represented to be: the story of Howard Hughes in the words of Howard Hughes himself.

Frank McCulloch (Bureau Chief, Time-Life News Services, who had met Howard Hughes):

> I am convinced beyond reasonable doubt as to the authenticity of the Howard Hughes autobiography. This conviction is based upon my long-standing personal familiarity with Howard Hughes, my reading of the manuscript and my interviews with Clifford Irving.

Ralph Graves (Managing Editor, *Life* Magazine):

> I respectfully submit that the unanimous opinion of highly respected journalists, the handwriting analysis of three of the foremost examiners of questioned documents, and the unhesitating conclusion reached by Mr. McCulloch can leave no reasonable doubt that the Howard Hughes autobiography is authentic and was authorized by him.

I was not at all surprised when Altman told me to catch the next United flight back to New York. This impossible conflict just had to be resolved.

I arrived in New York in the afternoon of January 20th and immediately checked into the Americana Hotel. There, at the message desk, I found a note telling me to stay put and not to come over to McGraw-Hill until the following day. I later learned the reason why. At that very moment, in the McGraw-Hill offices, Clifford Irving was attempting to explain to McGraw-Hill and Time-Life editors his theory regarding a new and most disquieting development taking place in Zurich, Switzerland. Investigators had discovered that the "H. R. Hughes" who endorsed and deposited $650,000 in a Swiss bank account was, in fact, a petite, German-speaking blond who was definitely not Howard Hughes, nor did she resemble any other members of Hughes's retinue. Could Irving shed any light on this unusual situation? As usual, Irving's manner was so disarming and his theories about the love interests in Hughes's life so plausible that nobody at the time thought to consider that the description of "H. R. Hughes" given by Swiss bank authorities also fit Clifford Irving's wife Edith.

The following morning of January 21st I taxied the short distance from my hotel to the McGraw-Hill building on 42nd Street. Weighted down with heavy bags of traveling examination equipment, I struggled into the elevator and up to an area in the book section where I

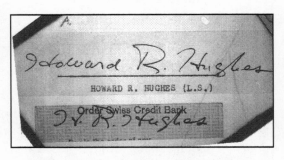

Forged Howard R. Hughes signature on check deposited in Swiss bank account.

114

was to conduct my examination. I was pleased to see that advance preparations had been made for my visit. All of the originals of questioned and exemplar documents were laid out for my examination on a large table with plenty of room at one end for my microscope, cameras, measuring instruments, and lighting equipment. I took a quick glance at the documents and couldn't help but notice that all of the handwritten letters in the stack marked "Questioned" were written on yellow, legal-size paper—the same kind of paper Hughes was known to use for virtually all communications. Under the caption "Howard Hughes Known" was the original of the "Dear Chester and Bill" letter submitted earlier in photographic form (and as a *Life* magazine reproduction). It, too, was written on yellow, legal-size paper. "Let me know when you are finished," said Mr. Cooke, my McGraw-Hill contact, as he prepared to leave the room. "Mr. Altman's partner, Mr. Dressel, wants you to call him with your final opinion before you go back to your hotel."

I pulled my stereoscopic microscope from its case, set up a portable light, and prepared for this new "adventure" of searching for answers in the inconspicuous details of handwriting purporting to be that of Howard Hughes. And they weren't long in coming. The *o*'s, *a*'s, *d*'s, and *g*'s in Hughes's known writings all started with almost imperceptible "fishhook" formations inside the ovals. The same letters in the autobiography writings did not. Other violations of Hughes's inconspicuous writing habits also became evident under the microscope—blunt rather than tapering beginning and ending strokes, tiny jogs in unusual areas of the lines indicative of two joined strokes, and pressure points in various areas of the strokes. So many things were revealed under my microscope that the day slipped away before I noticed it. Finally, using a 35mm color camera with a macro lens designed to produce

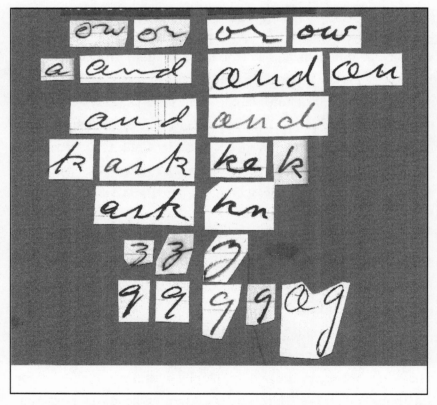

Left: Enlarged examples of Hughes's known writing showing delicate hooks inside the *o*'s, *a*'s, and double stroke *k*. Right: Clifford Irving failed to see and incorporate these inconspicuous characteristics into his forgeries.

greatly magnified images on the film, I photographed all of the areas I had examined under the microscope. I then went to the phone and called attorney Henry Dressel.

"The evidence is overwhelming that all of the autobiography documents submitted for my examination are spurious, contrived instruments," I said emphatically. "I would classify them all as expert forgeries."

To my surprise, Dressel reacted with none of the emotion displayed by his partner at the time I first gave him the shocking news. "Thank you, Mr. Doud," he merely said, "we will contact you tomorrow regarding a written report." What was going on in Dressel's mind? I really couldn't tell.

The four-page report I drafted in Milwaukee on January 24th reiterated my opinion that all of the writings I had examined were forged, adding, "Some of the less conspicuous and obviously difficult-to-imitate details of the writing were also violated. These included delicately retraced strokes, small loops and hooks in certain letters, relationship of one portion of a letter to another and placement of punctuations."

It took a second trip to New York on January 26th to apparently convince two different firms of McGraw-Hill lawyers that my conclusions were correct. This trip was memorable from several standpoints. Trial lawyers for McGraw-Hill had set up a moot-court arrangement to test the validity of the expert conclusions—placing the experts and the lawyers in an adversarial relationship familiar to them both. In this case, however, no judge was present to rule on any of the questions put to the witnesses, which was probably just as well. All questions, as far as I was concerned, were entirely proper from a legal standpoint and were designed to uncover the facts and not impugn the witnesses' impartiality or ability, as might have been true in some courts of law and with some unscrupulous lawyers.

I listened to the testimony of the first questioned document examiner employed by McGraw-Hill, who testified to the obvious pictorial similarities between Hughes's handwriting and that on the autobiography documents. As I recall, he used no comparison exhibits, only photographs of the documents themselves—high contrast photographs. Anxious to try out their newly learned cross-examination skills, the young lawyers obviously had a hard time attacking the expert's findings because of the pictorial similarities between Hughes's exemplar handwriting and the autobiography writings. The two *looked* the same.

When my turn came, I explained that what we were dealing with here was a skillful forgery of Hughes's writing. Then, using a handful of enlarged comparison charts, I showed the young lawyers how the forger failed to duplicate the inconspicuous details of Hughes's writing and missed several more prominent features of his writing as well. At the conclusion of my testimony, I would have to say, immodestly, that there was little room left for cross-examination. The impact of my comparison exhibits was so great that I could sense the gradual change in attitude of those young lawyers from one of skepticism to complete conviction that

Clifford Irving's autobiography documents were spurious. I left New York shortly thereafter feeling good about my part in this unusual exercise, pitting experts employed by the same company against each other. Shortly thereafter, McGraw-Hill and *Life* magazine discontinued all efforts to publish Clifford Irving's notorious Howard Hughes autobiography.

I like to think that my early warnings about Clifford Irving's fraudulent autobiography had something to do with this decision of McGraw Hill and Time-Life. It might even have saved them from a damaging and costly lawsuit by the Hughes corporate interests. Unfortunately, I could not save them from the embarrassment of being hoaxed by one of the cleverest forgers I have every encountered.

But what about this master conniver and forger, Clifford Irving? Following my last trip to New York, things began to go badly for him. It all started with an unexpected admission, made in the mistaken belief that the Swiss connection who endorsed the checks was about to be unmasked, that "H. R. Hughes" was Helga R. Hughes, was Edith Irving. From that moment on, everything was downhill for Clifford Irving. Fatal flaws were found in accounts of his world-wide meetings with Howard Hughes. For example, the Baroness Nina van Palandt disclosed that she and "Cliffy" were staying at the Hotel Victoria in Oaxaca, Mexico, at the time he was supposed to be taping interviews with Hughes. Scuba diving instructor Ann Baxter, who accompanied Irving to St. Croix, Virgin Islands, testified that it would have been impossible for him to meet with Hughes because she and Irving spent all of the time together scuba diving, dune buggy riding, or sightseeing.

Besieged from all sides, Clifford Irving finally crumbled under intense questioning by investigators for McGraw-Hill and Time-Life and admitted every detail of his attempt to bilk the publishers. A short time later, Irving, his wife Edith, and Richard Suskind, a surprising third participant in the scheme and co-author of the autobiography itself, were subpoenaed to appear before state and federal grand juries to hear a number of charges against them. Ultimately, all three pleaded guilty to charges of criminal possession of forged instruments, grand larceny, conspiracy, mail fraud, and, in the case of Irving alone, forgery.

It was this last count of forgery against Irving that created the biggest stir, for virtually no one believed that he alone had the ability to forge the autobiography documents. It just had to be Elmyr de Hory, "The World's Greatest Art Forger." After all, Clifford Irving had written a book about de Hory's ability to forge paintings and the signatures on them. But the artist vehemently denied any connection with the forgeries and produced convincing eyewitness proof that he could not have been involved.

In the meantime, Clifford Irving, who must have been amused at the refusal of some to believe his confession, proceeded to demonstrate, for the benefit of prosecutors and defense attorneys alike, his ability to forge Howard Hughes's writing. Using a pad of ruled paper, Irving quickly dashed off *from memory* the contents of the second letter giving him permission to write Howard Hughes's autobiography. The similarity to Hughes's genuine writing was unmistakable. He then proceeded to write a second version of the letter with the same freedom and speed with which he had written the first. There could be no mistake, Clifford Irving, and no one else, was the forger of the Hughes autobiography documents!

On June 16, 1972, before United States District Judge John M. Cannellas of the Southern District of New York, Clifford Irving was sentenced to two-and-a-half years imprisonment. Edith Irving received a sentence of two years, all but two months of which were suspended. Later that same day, District Judge Joseph Martinis sentenced Richard Suskind, the co-author of the "autobiography" to six months' imprisonment. Thus ended one of the most fascinating chapters in the annals of criminal jurisprudence. But the Prince of Thieves had one more arrow in his quiver. He would write a tell-all book.

Epilogue — Letting It All Hang Out

In the ninety days between pleading guilty to state and federal charges and his sentencing, Clifford Irving wrote a book about the Hughes autobiography hoax titled *What Really Happened*.[1] Richard Suskind was again listed as collaborator. This 378-page book is

---

1. Clifford Irving, with Richard Suskind. *What Really Happened: His Untold Story of the Hughes Affair* (New York: Grove Press, 1972).

remarkable not only for the speed with which it was written, but for its astonishing revelations about every aspect of the plot to hoax McGraw-Hill. Included in great detail was information on the planning and execution of the forgeries that later became the subject of my own examination. Viewed in the light of some of the problems I encountered, these disclosures represented absolutely fascinating reading.

Irving's book refers to only one signature forgery, the one on the contract, but this is revealing of his method of writing a signature over and over again until he achieved the desired results:

> I typed the final draft on white legal-size onionskin until I could see exactly how far down the final page the signatures should go. Then I signed 'Howard R. Hughes' on about fifty sheets in the correct place. 'Pick out the best three,' I told Dick [Richard Suskind], handing him *Life*'s reproduction of the letter to Chester Davis and Bill Gay for comparison.

Irving's last statement regarding the signature to the "Chester and Bill" reprint being used as the model for his signature forgeries is hard to accept. If that is true, why did he insert a pen lift between the *o* and *w* that was not in the *Life* reproduction? That is an enigma to which I have yet to find an answer. The use of the abbreviated signature "H. R. Hughes" is more explainable. Edith Irving couldn't very well deposit in a Swiss bank account McGraw-Hill checks payable to "Howard R. Hughes."

As expected, the forgeries of fourteen pages of cursive writings gave Irving the biggest challenge. Telling about his first attempt to copy from the short *Newsweek* example, Irving states:

> I went over it [the *Newsweek* example] carefully, analyzing the lower-case letters first and then the capital letters. Fortunately the paragraph contained specimens of all but six lower-case letters: *b, j, k, q, x,* and *z.* It would be hard to write a letter without a *b*, but Hughes seemed to base his handwriting on the standard form of penmanship taught when I was in grammar school, so I could keep the *b*'s to the minimum, fake them, and hope for the best. To my horror, however, I realized immediately that the sample I had to work from gave me only five capital letters: *A, I, M, H,* and *R.* The major problem therefore, was to create a correspondence using only those capital letters. I mulled that for a few minutes and then hit on the simplest solution. Hughes would be the supreme egotist. He would begin every possible sentence in his letters with the pronouns I and My…The next day I…drafted the three Hughes letters *on my typewriter.* I made a few changes to eliminate all unnecessary capital letters with which I was unfamiliar, then called Dick in Palma. I read the letters aloud. "Not bad,' he said. "But a little stiff.' 'Howard's not a writer,' I pointed out. 'That's why he needs me to do his biography.'

Irving's task became much easier when he learned of the two-page *Life* version, which he ultimately used as the model for his forgeries. The sample included thirteen capitals and all of the small letters except the *z*. Regarding that lucky find, Irving writes:

> I had gone over the three letters from Howard to me, comparing them once again with the letter reproduced in *Life*, and decided that my second version was passable but hardly expert. I spent two days drafting still a third version, giving up only when I had run out of yellow legal paper. That was it, I decided, as I reproduced all the doodles and stains that appeared on the second version.

One emerges from reading *What Really Happened* with a grudging admiration for the intelligence and persistence of Clifford Irving, Prince of Thieves, who almost pulled off the greatest hoax of the twentieth century.

But the story does not end here. Three newspaper reporters, Stephen Fay, Lewis Chester, and Magnus Linklater, who had become interested in events surrounding the Hughes autobiography dispute, teamed up in late 1972 to write a book titled *Hoax: The Inside Story of the Howard Hughes-Clifford Irving Affair*.[1]

Five years after the publication of *Hoax: The Inside Story of the*

---

1. Stephen Fay, Lewis Chester, and Magnus Linklater, *Hoax: The Inside Story of the Howard Hughes-Clifford Irving Affair* (New York: The Viking Press, 1972).

Howard Hughes-Clifford Irving Affair, as unbelievable as it may seem, the book *Hoax* became the centerpiece of another, even more ambitious plot—this time to bilk the estate of Howard Hughes. Again the handwriting played an important part in the resolution of the case, and I was one of the questioned document examiners employed by heirs of the Hughes estate to examine what became known as the "Mormon Will" of Howard Hughes.

6

Howard Hughes:
Mormon Will Case

Hoaxed Again in the Hereafter

'I quite agree with you,' said the Duchess, 'and the moral of that is: Be what you would seem to be, or if you'd like it put more simply: Never imagine yourself not to be otherwise than what it might appear to others that what you were or might have been was not otherwise than what you had been would have appeared to them to be otherwise.'

LEWIS CARROLL, *Alice's Adventures in Wonderland*

"Well, there it is, Mr. Doud," said the Las Vegas District Court Clerk, handing me a large sealed envelope, "the most examined document in the United States. That old son-of-a-bitch is probably up there—or down there—laughing his head off at all the commotion caused by this alleged Mormon will of his."

Having observed Hughes's indignant reaction five years earlier to the forged autobiography documents produced by Clifford Irving, I doubted that even in the hereafter he would have found much to laugh about in the current attempt to hoax his estate. As far as I was concerned, the strange documents I pulled from that envelope were more pathetic than amusing.

Encased between sheets of one-half inch clear plastic attached at the corners by screws, the three pages of the Mormon will were as highly protected as the Constitution of the United States. But there the similarity ended. Nobody could ever mistake that illiterate, smudged, and childlike scribbling for anything written by this country's most honored patriots, or Howard Hughes for that matter. It looked terrible. When I compared the writing with a small sampling of Hughes's genuine writing handed me by the clerk, the differences were so obvious as to be almost laughable.

My thoughts returned to the genuine writings of Howard Hughes I had examined in the Clifford Irving case. Was there anything about them to indicate some deterioration in Hughes's handwriting around March 19, 1968, the date appearing on the will? Despite the passage of five years, I could still recall every detail of Hughes's writing, and there was nothing in 1968 or any other time remotely resembling the writings on this document.

Using hand magnifiers of various powers, the handwriting looked even worse. Despite the difficulty of conducting an examination through one-half inch thick plastic sheeting, I could find scarcely a letter that wasn't patched up, slowly written, or badly aligned. The track of the pen wavered here and there and reflected in every possible way the painful manner in which the strokes were made.

To add to the document's wretched appearance, a liquid of some sort had been spilled on selected parts of all three pages, which made the ball pen inks run and stain the paper. Based upon the areas affected by the liquid, it looked to me like a deliberate attempt by the forger to obscure some of his mistakes. Adding to the Kafkaesque nature of the evidence, the paper of the inner envelope in which the will was enclosed was brittle around the edges and had all the appearance of being baked in an oven to give it the aura of age—too much age for a document dated in 1968.

Although I always try to avoid making snap judgments, I could not help thinking to myself, "This is ridiculous—what am I doing here examining a document that anyone in his right mind can see is a forgery? The courts will throw it out, and the perpetrator of the fraud will be prosecuted, and that will end the matter."

But my prognosis couldn't have been more wrong. What should have been a simple case that most judges would have decided from the bench or in chambers developed into a major legal battle costing litigants for both sides millions of dollars in fees and expenses. All told, it took one and one-half years of investigative work by attorneys, questioned document examiners, and others working for both "Proponent" (side supporting the Mormon will) and "Contestants" (Estate of Howard Hughes contesting the will) plus seven months of trial before the case was finally adjudicated. In the process, the reputations of certain institutions named in the Mormon will suffered irreparable damage, not to speak of several witnesses who either perjured themselves or testified against the facts.

The Mormon will case had its beginning in the headquarters building of the Church of Jesus Christ of Latter-Day Saints, Salt Lake City, Utah. The date was April 27, 1976. On returning to his office after an afternoon break, one of the church information specialists found lying on his desk a bulky white envelope on the outside of which was written in backhanded script:

President Spencer W. Kimball
Church of Jesus Christ
Salt Lake City, Utah

Outer envelope, delivered to Mormon officials on April 27, 1976.

When Rosemary Applegate, President Kimball's secretary, opened the outer envelope, she found inside a tan envelope of some apparent age plus a separate scrap of white paper bearing the words in the same backhanded script as the outer envelope:

This was found by Joseph F. Smith's house in 1972
Thought you would be interested.

Note left with the will. Dummar later admitted this was his handwriting.

On the front of the tan envelope was written:
Dear Mr. Mckay
please see that this Will
is delivered after my death to
Clark County Court House,
Las Vagas Nevada.

Inner envelope, containing Howard Hughes's purported will.

131

Upon opening this envelope, Rosemary Applegate found three pages of stained, yellow legal pad paper on which was handwritten the purported last will and testament of Howard Hughes.

Last Will and Testament

I Howard R. Hughes being of
sound and disposing mind and
memory, not acting under duress,
fraud or the undue influence
of any person whomsoever,
and being a resident of Las Vegas,
Nevada, declare that this
is to be my last Will
and Revolk all other wills
previously made by me —

After my death my estate
is to be devided as follows —

first: one forth of all my assets to go to Hughes Med-
ical Institute of Miami

second: one eight of assets
to be devided among
the University of Texas —
Rice Institute of Technology
of Houston —
 the University of Nevada —
and the University of Calif.

  Howard R. Hughes
  --page one—

Last Will and Testament

I Howard R. Hughes being of sound and disposing mind and memory, not acting under duress, fraud or the undue influence of any person whomsoever, and being a resident of Las Vegas Nevada. declare that this is to be my last Will and revolk all other willes previously made by me –

After my death my estate is to be devided as follows:–

first: one forth of all my assets to go to Hughes Medical Institute of Miami –

second: one eight of assets to be devided among the University of Texas Rice Institute of Technology of Houston – the University of Nevada. and the University of Calif.

Howard R. Hughs

– page one –

Page 1 of Howard Hughes's purported will.

third: one sixteenth to Church
of Jesus Christ of Latterday
Saints – David O. McKay - Pre

Forth: one sixteenth to establish a home for Orphan
Cildren –

Fifth: one sixteenth of assets
to go to Boy Scouts
of America

Sixth: one sixteenth: to be
devided among Jean Peters of
Los Angeles and Ella Rice
of Houston –

seventh: one sixteenth of assets
to William R. Lommis of
Houston, Texas –

eighth: one sixteenth to go
to Melvin De Mar of
Gabbs Nevada –

        Howard R. Hughes
   –page two–

third: one sixteenth to Church
of Jesus Christ of Latterday
Saints — David O. McKay Pre

Forth: one sixteenth to establish a home for Orphan
Children —

Fifth: one sixteenth of assets
to go to Boy Scouts
of America.

sixth: one sixteenth: to be
divided among Jean Peters of
Los Angeles and Ella Rice
of Houston —

seventh: one sixteenth of assets
to William R. Lommis of
Houston, Texas —

eighth: one sixteenth to go
to Melvin Du Mar of
Gabbs Nevada —

Howard R. Hughes

— page two —

Page 2 of Howard Hughes's purported will.

ninth: one sixteenth to be
devided among my
personal aids at the time
of my death —

tenth: one sixteenth to be
 used as school scholarship
fund for entire country —

the spruce goose is to be given
to the City of Long Beach Calif—

the remainder of my
estate is to be devided among
the key men of the company's
I own at the time of my death.

I appoint Noah Dietrich
as the executor of this Will —

  signed the 19 day of
  March 1968

  Howard R. Hughes
--page three

ninth; one sixteenth to be
devided among my
personal aids at the time
of my death —

tenth; one sixteenth to be
used as school scholarship
fund for entire Country —

The spruce goose is to be given
to the City of Long Beach, Calif

The remainder of My
estate is to be devided among
the key men of the company's
I own at the time of my
death.

I appoint Noah Dietrich
as the executer of this will —

signed the 19 day of
March 1968

Howard R. Hughes

— page three —

Page 3 of Howard Hughes's purported will.

Investigators for the Hughes interests as well as the ever-present media were immediately attracted to the bequest at the bottom of page two: "eighth: one sixteenth to go to Melvin Du Mar of Gabbs Nevada." With but two or three exceptions, the other bequests to the Hughes Medical Institute; the four different universities; charities such as the Boy Scouts of America; his pride and joy, the *Spruce Goose*—the largest aircraft ever to be built; aides and business associates; and the Mormon Church, seemed to be reasonably consistent with the way Howard Hughes might have wanted his estate divided. But who was this Melvin Du Mar and why was he a beneficiary under the Mormon will?

When Melvin Dummar (the name "Du Mar" was misspelled in the will) was finally located at his gas station in Willard, Utah, he had a wonderful and imaginative tale to spin about an unusual encounter with Howard Hughes: Sometime in January of 1968, according to Dummar's story, he got into his 1966 blue, two-door Chevrolet Caprice, planning to make the eight-hour trip from Gabbs, Nevada, where he lived at that time, to Las Vegas, following which he would visit his daughter who lived in Cypress, California. Driving south towards Las Vegas on a lonely stretch of Route 95, Dummar pulled off the highway onto a rutted shoulder of the road, planning to relieve himself and rest for a short period of time. He had gone approximately one hundred yards when his headlights picked up the figure of a man lying on his stomach in the middle of the road. As described by Dummar, the subject creature whom he helped to his feet was more than six feet tall, skinny, and over sixty years old. He was wearing a sport shirt, slacks, and a pair of tennis shoes. There was dried blood all over the shirt from blood coming out of his left ear. "My immediate reaction," said Dummar, "was that someone had beat up the old man and dumped him there."

Helping the pitiful creature into his car, Dummar told of continuing on his way to Las Vegas. During the journey, his passenger seemed dazed and had little to say, with but one exception. In response to Dummar's off-the-cuff remark that he once applied for a job at Hughes Aircraft, his passenger allegedly commented, "I am familiar with Hughes Aircraft because I own the company. I am Howard Hughes." Dummar said he snickered at that statement coming from someone obviously suffering from delusions.

When they arrived in Las Vegas, Dummar's passenger reportedly asked to be let out at the Sands Hotel. After introducing himself as Melvin Dummar of Gabbs, Nevada, he was surprised to hear the old man again reiterate that he was Howard Hughes. In parting, according to Dummar's story, he handed him some change, ostensibly to make a telephone call, and Hughes responded, "Thank you, Melvin."

A revisionary movie version of the case called "Melvin and Howard" was produced sometime after the conclusion of the Mormon will trial. Illustrative of how Hollywood distorts events and historical facts to suit their own warped views of reality, this movie makes a hero of Melvin Dummar and villains of "the establishment" that exposed Dummar's duplicity. In the movie version, Hughes was riding a motorcycle in the desert when he has an unfortunate accident. Melvin finds him badly bruised and bleeding and becomes his Good Samaritan.

Driving a rusty old pickup truck on his way to Las Vegas, because that is Hollywood's vision of the model of transportation used by poverty-stricken victims of societal injustice, Dummar tries to get his passenger to loosen up and become a kindred free spirit. As a self-styled country singer and composer, Melvin introduces Hughes to one of his own compositions, which he sings a couple of times as they drive along the highway. First by coaxing, then by implied threat, Melvin induces Hughes to join him in singing a wonderful new ballad he has just composed titled "Santa's Souped Up Sleigh." In the end, Hughes is won over into the anti-establishment attitude espoused by Dummar. When they arrive in Las Vegas, the Good Samaritan drops his grateful new friend off at the Sands Hotel with a smile and a gift of twenty-five cents. How unselfish of Melvin to give this wretched man the last coin in his pocket, and how generous of Howard Hughes to return the favor with a Mormon will bequest of $156,000,000!!

While not quite as imaginative as the movie version, Dummar's own story was equally hard to believe and presented problems to those hoping to establish the legitimacy of the Mormon will. Not only did the desert encounter with Howard Hughes seem unbelievable, but after denying several times under oath that he knew anything about the Mormon will, Dummar finally admitted that he was the one who delivered the envelope containing the will to Mormon Church headquarter in Salt Lake City, Utah. The sudden stab of conscience that prompted Dummar to change his story was, no doubt, aided by a report from the FBI stating that a fingerprint found on the outer envelope was his. When Lyndal Shaneyfelt, one of Contestants' experts, identified him as the writer of the backhanded script on both the outer envelope and accompanying note, Dummar finally admitted that this was also true. But in answer to the most important question of all, Dummar was adamant. "No suh, ah didn't write that will," he said.

Another fingerprint of Dummar's was found on a copy of the book *Hoax* located in the reference library at Weber State College, Utah, where Dummar had taken a few courses. Written by three Canadian authors four years earlier, *Hoax* described the incredible story of the Clifford Irving-Howard Hughes autobiography scam in which I was employed by McGraw-Hill to examine certain disputed signatures and handwritten letters. In the centerfold section were sixteen pages of illustrations including photos of Howard Hughes; his aides; his ex-wives and love interests; the *Spruce Goose*, the world's largest airplane; and, of course, Clifford Irving, his co-conspirators, and his McGraw-Hill victims. Also included was a one-page reprint of the "Chester and Bill" letter in *Life*, and two "interrogatory" signatures of Howard Hughes signed to questions posed by reporters.

All of the illustrations had been torn out of the Weber State copy of *Hoax,* including the specimens of Hughes's handwriting.

During one of Dummar's depositions, he admitted to looking at the Weber State copy "for the sake of curiosity," but denied having torn out the centerfold pages for any purpose.

A few weeks after Dummar's deposition, an opportunity arose for me to examine the Weber State copy of *Hoax*, which was then in the possession of the District Attorney in Carson City, Nevada. My purpose was to see if I could find any evidence connecting Melvin Dummar's fingerprint to the act of tearing out the centerfold pages—a connection that would have impeached Dummar's testimony. I could find none, but based upon the mangled strings in the book's binding, it was obvious that someone had torn out the illustrative section of *Hoax* in a big hurry.

With Dummar's stories changing almost on a daily basis, the Mormon will controversy should have suffered an inglorious death, not only from the sheer weight of Dummar's lies but from testimony by Hughes's "Palace Guards" that he was physically incapable of escaping from his self-imposed, prison-like existence in the Desert Inn. Not only were all exits from his suite of rooms heavily guarded, but even if he managed to slip past the guards, his emaciated 100-pound body would not have had the energy to walk miles into the desert. But there was no escaping the sad realities of life in the twentieth century. There was just too much money at stake, too much searching for power, and too much Mormon Church influence to let the Mormon will die.

The ensuing case essentially boiled down to one question: Did Howard Hughes write the three page Mormon will and

142

accompanying envelope or were the documents forged? The battle lines were drawn when Noah Dietrich, named as executor on page three of the Mormon will, appointed Attorney Harold Rhoden of Beverly Hills, California, to act as substitute executor and to proceed as counsel for Proponent of the will. Rhoden, a short-statured, aggressive, and cunning advocate, was assisted from time to time by others seeking to bask in the light of media publicity, including "palimony" lawyer Marvin Mitchelson.

Financing for Proponent's case, so it was said, was provided by Seymour Lazar, a wealthy Los Angeles stock market speculator, and by Harold Rhoden, who borrowed from his friends and mortgaged most of his property to raise the required funds. Despite reports from their own questioned document experts that the Mormon will was a forgery, the Universities of Texas, California, Rice, and the Boy Scouts of America agreed to pay jury fees and the substantial costs of daily transcripts. I was sickened when one of Contestants' attorneys told me of this arrangement, especially as it related to Rice University, which was founded by William Marsh Rice, a blood relative of Hughes's. Contestant Annette Gano Lummis from Houston and other members of her family were also blood relatives of William Marsh Rice and had contributed literally millions of dollars throughout the years to support Rice University. Helping to finance the trial of a will the University had every reason to believe was a forgery seemed like an odd way of expressing thanks to the Lummis family.

On Contestants' side were attorneys James Dilworth and

Clayton Lilienstern representing Summa, the Hughes holding corporation, and Annette Gano Lummis, Hughes's aunt and closest heir on the maternal side, residing in Houston, Texas. Also appearing for Contestants was attorney Paul Freese of Los Angeles, representing three second cousins on Hughes's paternal side. Under the laws of intestacy, if the Mormon Will was disallowed, the maternal and paternal heirs would receive the bulk of Hughes's estate.

I was employed by the maternal heir; Lyndal Shaneyfelt, former FBI examiner was employed by Summa Corp.; John J. Harris, questioned document examiner from Los Angeles, was employed by the paternal heirs. Unlike Proponent, Contestants paid all of their own expenses relating to the will contest—expenses that were borne equally by the Texas and California heirs.

But the three of us were not the only questioned document examiners employed to examine the Mormon will. In fact, the case became a convocation of experts, with fifteen handwriting experts being consulted by Proponent, three by Contestants, two more by institutions named in the will, one by the State of Nevada, and one by ABC television. When the District Court clerk told me at the time of our first meeting that the Mormon will was "the most examined document in the United States" he wasn't just kidding.

As it turned out, there was a great deal of attrition in the ranks of Proponent's experts, most of whom correctly reported to Harold Rhoden that the Mormon will was a forgery. The institutions named in the will also received reports from their experts stating that the will was spurious, as did the State of Nevada.

Ultimately, Proponent was left with four experts, two from France, one from Holland, and one from the United States, all of whom were prepared to testify that the Mormon will was genuine. Three had graphological backgrounds, a type of training unacceptable to those of us in public and private practice who were trained scientifically. The fourth expert, Henri Ollivier of France, had the most unusual background of all. As described in his testimony, he was both a doctor of medicine and a doctor of police science as well as an expert in the detection of forgery in documents. I couldn't help but wonder how this busy man had time to sleep.

Would any of Proponent's four experts have been able to meet the requirements of the American Board of Forensic Document Examiners, the certifying arm of the profession in the United States? I doubted it. Yet, despite their questionable training, all three of the European experts had acted, in one capacity or another, as official advisors to the courts of justice in their respective countries. Presumably, this meant their opinions were accepted by the courts without question and without cross-examination. Based upon the awful mistake they made in the Mormon will case, one is led to question the logic of a legal system so dependent upon the conclusions of its own experts but so careless about their qualifications.

Contestants ended up with the same questioned document experts they started with: Harris, Shanneyfelt, and Doud. Without appearing to be immodest, the qualifications of the three of us were like day is to night compared to those of Proponent's experts.

Back in the Las Vegas District Clerk's office I was faced with a dilemma. How far should I go in examining a document that, even on brief inspection, was such an obvious forgery?

The attorneys for the estate of Howard Hughes answered that question. "If the Mormon will is a forgery, as you believe it to be, Mr. Doud, you must be prepared to prove it beyond a reasonable doubt."

But how should I continue? At the time of my initial examination, hand magnifiers were perfectly satisfactory for viewing evidence through the one-half inch plastic protective sheeting, but the use of a stereoscopic microscope was almost impossible. Moreover, any attempt to photograph the handwriting with my 4 x 5 fixed focus box camera was certain to produce an out-of-focus image. I just had to obtain permission from the court to remove the plastic covering.

Earlier in the day I had appeared before Judges Waite and Thompson of the Las Vegas Probate and District Courts to swear that I would not alter or change the evidence in any way during the course of my examination. So it was back to Judge Thompson to again plead my case. Yes, I could remove the plastic covers, but I must use surgical gloves to conduct my examination of the Mormon will and envelope because the documents had not as yet been tested for fingerprints. So be it!

Fortunately, I did not have to go through this same procedure in examining Hughes's known writing consisting of several memos of various dates written on yellow legal pad paper to one of his attorneys. They could be handled with impunity.

When I asked the District Court Clerk about the original "Chester and Bill" letter (referred to at the subsequent trial as the "C and B" letter), I was told the document was unavailable, having been subpoenaed for a federal court case in Los Angeles involving Summa, the Hughes holding company. Neither did the Clerk have copies of the two-page *Life* reproduction of "C and B" or the later one-page reprint in *Hoax*.

Before leaving Milwaukee for Las Vegas, I had reviewed copies of "C and B" from *Hoax* and *Life* and was tempted to bring them along with me. I was glad that I did not, because several weeks later during a pre-trial deposition in Milwaukee conducted by Attorney Rhoden, I was cross-examined about using my Irving case copies of the "C and B" letter for the Mormon will examination. Rhoden seemed to imply that this would have been inappropriate from a legal standpoint, although for the life of me I couldn't see why. My answer to his question was, "No, I did not bring the Irving case copies to Las Vegas," but he didn't ask me about my *memory* of "C and B," which was as vivid as when I had first examined the original and its *Life* reproduction during the Clifford Irving case. How could I forget? I had spent countless hours tabulating capital and small letters in the *Life* version and comparing them with the five autobiography letters supposedly written by Hughes.

For purposes of the Mormon will examination, the genuine

Howard Hughes specimens submitted by the Clerk of Courts were more than adequate and reinforced my initial impression that the Mormon will was a crude forgery. I had found glaring differences in every aspect of the script, including skill of writing, letter forms, size, spacing, and slant. Under the microscope, the writings looked even worse, with most strokes being written in a tremorous, unnatural fashion exactly the opposite of Hughes's free-flowing script.

My long-time friend and fellow expert Jack Harris, who was the first of Contestants' experts to examine the Mormon will, announced to the press following his examination that the Mormon will was "a rank forgery." Counsel for Contestants gave Jack permission to make that statement, hoping thereby to focus media attention on this crude attempt to bilk the Howard Hughes estate. Unfortunately, it did not accomplish its intended goal, and at the subsequent trial, Jack was vigorously cross-examined about expressing such a fast conclusion. I, too, found the Mormon will to be "a rank forgery," but managed to avoid the press by dodging out the back door of the courthouse.

The question of whether or not the forger used the "C and B" reprints in *Life* or *Hoax* from which to copy the Mormon will writing was something I could best deal with in my Milwaukee laboratory. In the meantime, my rough count of twenty-two different capitals being used in the Mormon will and my *memory* of only thirteen in the *Life* and *Hoax* reproductions suggested some interesting possibilities.

Counsel for Contestants had now scheduled a meeting in Los Angeles to discuss the final results of my Las Vegas examination and various aspects of the impending trial. So I bid farewell to the clanking slot machines and sleazy atmosphere of the Las Vegas gambling scene, checked out of the Sands Hotel, and headed for the airport to take the next flight to Los Angeles.

Upon arriving in the city where I had spent most of my early youth, I immediately taxied over to the offices of attorney Paul Freese, whom I had not met before, and then to the spacious office and laboratory of Jack Harris. Jack hadn't changed much since the early days when I worked for Clark Sellers and he for his father, John L. Harris, in an office directly across Spring Street. Slender, vigorous, and with a receding hairline about which he worried a lot, Jack was a highly qualified questioned document examiner. His easy, informal manner, retentive memory, and piercing tenor voice also made him a formidable witness in court. The conference arranged in Harris's office also afforded me the opportunity of meeting face-to-face all three of Contestants' attorneys.

Lead attorney for the maternal heir was James Dilworth, gruff, middle-aged, heavy-set lawyer from the Houston law firm of Andres, Kurth, Campbell & Jones. His firm had performed much of Hughes's work in the past as well as that of the Summa Corporation. Clayton Lilienstern, Dilworth's junior partner in the case, was his direct opposite. Handsome, poised, and flashing a charismatic smile, Lilienstern, a man in his early forties, could easily have been the prototype for television's Perry Mason. I had the feeling that at any future trial the women on the jury would like Clay Lilienstern—a lot!

Paul Freese, a slender, greying man of medium stature, impressed me as being a trial lawyer of keen intelligence and ability. I also liked him as a person. As might be expected in a case involving strong-minded trial attorneys, Freese sometimes differed with his Houston co-counsel on trial strategy, cross-examination of witnesses, and general conduct of the case. But as far as I could tell, they always managed to patch things up.

Among the subjects covered in our conference were the excuses Proponent might advance for the decrepit appearance of the Mormon will writings. One that was sure to be made was Hughes's kidney disease (renal failure), the effects of which caused his writing to deteriorate to a point where he could no longer control the pen, misspelled words, and made grammatical mistakes. To test the validity of that argument, Harris and I had instructed Contestants to search for Hughes specimens dated around March 19, 1968, the date appearing on the Mormon will.

To our delight, they produced a mother lode of contemporaneously dated writings including a memo dated just one day before March 19, 1968, and another four days later. I carefully examined these new specimens and could see no noticeable difference between them and the Hughes specimens I had examined in Las Vegas. Even with the implausible scenario that Hughes had suffered a sudden onset of kidney failure on March 19th from which he recovered four days later, the classic signs in the

Mormon will were not of illness but of forgery.

On the morning of my last day in Los Angeles, I packed up my examination equipment and taxied over to the federal court building to renew my acquaintanceship with the original "C and B" letter. I had last seen this document in the New York offices of McGraw-Hill during the Clifford Irving case.

The document produced by the federal court clerk was just as I had remembered it—three pages of yellow legal-pad paper bearing the firm, well-controlled handwriting of Howard Hughes. But the message itself was far from controlled, being a vituperative order from Hughes to Chester Davis and Bill Gay to fire Robert Maheu, head of Hughes's Nevada operations.

I spent the better part of that morning examining, or should I say reexamining, the "C and B" letter and making photographs. With that document and other Hughes specimens I had examined in Las Vegas and Los Angeles, there were now more than enough known writings to cover all possible exigencies—or so I thought. A simple case that started off with a handful of Hughes exemplars was about to become a terribly complicated one involving over 450 newly-found specimens. Contestants produced a few of these documents because of their content and to show Hughes's mental capacity (and ability to write) in March of 1968. But it was Proponent's lawyers who cherished them the most. And for what reason? They were desperately looking for letters that would match some of the odd-looking characters in the Mormon will, and they kept searching through more and more documents in an effort to

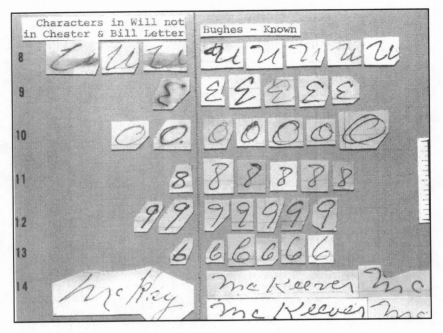

Comparison exhibit, consisting of juxtaposed examples of Hughes's known writings and thirteen characters in the questioned will that were not found in the Chester and Bill reproduction, and therefore would not be available for copying. The fundamental differences between questioned and known writings are so apparent as to leave little doubt that these characters were not written by Howard Hughes. Note in item 14 the discrepant positioning of the *c* of "McKay".

find them. Most were completely non-existent, much to the chagrin of the American expert and her three European counterparts, who later had great difficulty in explaining the discrepancies to the jury. Insofar as I was concerned, the introduction of 450 new Hughes memos was about to turn this case into a cataloging nightmare.

Back in my Milwaukee laboratory and now with the help of my

sons John and Bob, the films taken in Las Vegas and Los Angeles were processed and enlarged prints made from the negatives. Comparison exhibits, consisting of juxtaposed examples of Hughes's known writings and those on the Mormon will, were then pasted onto large sheets of illustration board, for study purposes. I also looked up my case file in the Clifford Irving-Howard Hughes autobiography affair and pulled out the two-page *Life* reprint of "C and B" similar to the one Irving admittedly used for his forgeries. In my library copy of the book *Hoax*, I turned to the illustrative section containing a second one-page version of "C and B" together with two reduced-size signatures of Hughes originally signed to "interrogatories" directed to him by the press at the time of the Irving fiasco.

The addition of the reprint evidence to all of the other writings I had examined in Las Vegas and Los Angeles resulted in the most astonishing diversity of proof I have ever encountered in any case. The Mormon will was indeed a "rank forgery," as Jack Harris had said, violating Hughes' writing habits in every conceivable way.

The trial to establish whether or not Howard Hughes wrote and signed the Mormon will began in Las Vegas on November 7, 1977, and ended seven months later on June 8, 1978. I was scheduled to testify as the last of the handwriting experts. As far as I was concerned, this scheduling was both bad news and good news. The bad news was that I had seven months to fret and stew over my testimony, knowing that when I finally took the witness stand the jury would probably be bored to death with the subject of handwriting and the Mormon will.

The good news was that, in the interim, Contestants' attorneys had asked me to be present in court to hear the testimony of Proponent's experts and to help prepare cross-examination questions for them. I wouldn't have missed that experience for the world. I wasn't as enthusiastic about the seven trips from Milwaukee to Las Vegas that I was required to make. On each occasion I was housed in some gambling casino, such as the Sands Hotel, and in the process developed a deep-seated dislike for Las Vegas and everything it represented.

Before the trial ever got started, a serious drama was being played out—one relating to the fitness of District Judge Keith Hayes to preside over the Mormon will trial. Hayes, a balding, serious man in his middle forties, had referred to the impending trial as "a high stakes search for the truth." The question posed by Contestants was whether he really could adhere to the latter part of that statement. Under the will, the Mormon Church was named as beneficiary of one-sixteenth of the Hughes estate. Therefore, it did seem unusual that Judge Hayes, a devout Mormon and bishop in the church, would so vigorously fight efforts by Contestants' attorneys to disqualify him on the basis of possible bias.

At one point, a telephone conversation between Proponent's attorney Rhoden and LeVane Forsythe, a character who portrayed himself as a bagman for Howard Hughes, was secretly recorded and played back to Judge Hayes. It was Harold Rhoden's voice, reassuring Forsythe that if he appeared as a witness in the case he would be on the winning side: "You don't have to worry about this Judge Hayes in Vegas," cajoled Rhoden. Forsythe replied, "Why don't I?" Rhoden continued, "He's a Mormon. Naturally, he wants the will admitted to probate. Christ, he'll welcome you with open arms! So, please, Lee, reconsider. A lot of us are counting on you."

Even this damaging evidence did not deter the judge in his fight to remain in the Mormon will trial. Citing testimonials by fellow judges that he was always fair and impartial in his rulings, even when the Mormon Church was involved, Judge Hayes eventually won his battle in the Nevada Supreme Court.

Another reason for wanting Judge Hayes removed from the case was a cancerous condition from which he had suffered for some time. The seriousness of his condition soon became apparent when, during the course of the trial, Judge Hayes was periodically forced to take time off for chemotherapy treatments. Indeed, during the last month of the trial, it became touch and go as to whether Judge Hayes would survive to the end. He died seventeen months after the jury verdict.

One morning when I appeared in court early to confer with Contestants' attorneys, I noticed a group of perhaps twenty to thirty youngsters sitting in the spectator area. To the surprise of both trial participants and spectators alike, the judge proudly announced to all present, "These are children from my Sunday school class whom I teach every week." Then, addressing the children, the judge said, "I wanted you young people to come down here to see how a court of law operates. Some of you might want to be judges or lawyers when you grow up."

Continuing with his monologue, Judge Hayes made it clear that there was a difference between his supreme role as judge and arbitrator and that of the attorneys who were paid advocates for their respective clients. "As you can see," he said, "I am the judge of this court, and it is my job to see that all of the rules are obeyed by the lawyers and witnesses." Then, pointing to Harold Rhoden, Proponent's lawyer, he said, "Now, this gentleman is here in court to try to prove that the Mormon will of Howard Hughes is genuine. The three gentlemen at that other table," pointing to Dilworth, Lilienstern, and Freese, "are trying to prove that somebody forged the handwriting on the Mormon will. I will help the jury with the legal part of the case, but they will have to decide which of the two sides to believe."

From my vantage point in the front row of the spectator's area, I was privy to everything going on in the courtroom, including happenings that would have done justice to a Gilbert and Sullivan comic opera. For example, Proponent's French expert, Pierre Faideau, had arrived in court early accompanied by his new wife, an attractive Algerian woman many years his junior. A slender, stooped, unkempt man in his mid-forties, Faideau had the pallor of a man who might not survive to the next day. That impression was enhanced when he immediately slumped into one of the chairs in the jury box and appeared to fall asleep. I secretly wondered if his new wife had worn him out the night before.

For the next few moments, the young bride enthusiastically

bounced and chattered around the almost empty courtroom apparently trying to inject a little enthusiasm into her husband, and finally ended up literally vaulting up the two stairs leading to the witness box. My understanding of French is very limited, but I did catch the drift of her remarks as she proudly sat in the witness chair and told her lethargic husband how it would feel to be the man-of-the-hour in such a famous case. "Do not be afraid, Pierre. You will soon be up here in this chair where I am sitting. Everyone will be watching you. How proud you will be to tell our family that you testified in the Howard Hughes Mormon will case."

Faideau could only speak French; and as I later listened to the translation of his feeble attempts to explain away the many discrepancies in the Mormon will writing, I was constrained to think that despite the poor command of English, his wife would have made a much better, and certainly much livelier, witness. The most memorable part of his testimony was at the end when he turned to Judge Hayes and said, "Your Honor, I thank you…for the privilege of being allowed to contribute what I could to what I have been told you have called a search for the truth." I am sure most of the people in the courtroom who listened to the translation of Faideau's testimony that day felt as I did that his contribution to "the search for the truth" was non-existent. Indeed, there was so little real substance to his testimony that I could offer only a few cross-examination questions to Clay Lilienstern, including one relating to his graphological background.

As Faideau was assisted out of the courtroom door by his

energetic young wife, I could only shake my head in disbelief at the effrontery of this strange little Frenchman to come to the United States and testify in support of a crude, obvious forgery. I wondered whether news of his wretched performance would ever get back to France.

Henri Ollivier, the second Frenchman to testify at the trial, also required a translator. A pompous, overweight man in his late sixties, Ollivier also tried to explain away all of the differences between Hughes's writing and the Mormon will. What he lacked in evidence he made up for in exaggerated superlatives such as, "There is no room, my good sir, for any doubt, even the smallest [as to the genuineness of the Mormon will]. I am certain, and on this certainty I would stake my life." In a private conversation quoted by Proponent's attorney Harold Rhoden, Ollivier was even more emphatic. "If anyone can prove me wrong, I will place my head on the guillotine." Fortunately for Ollivier, the only thing he lost in the case was his reputation. His testimony was so bad that Contestants' attorneys didn't even bother to cross-examine him.

I was not in the courtroom to hear the testimony of Proponent's sole American expert, but from all accounts she did more harm than good to their case. There were so many inconsistencies in her testimony that Proponent's attorney Harold Rhoden, in his closing argument, advised the jury to completely ignore her testimony. Never in my experience have I heard an attorney so completely disclaim the testimony of his own witness.

In order to provide the jury some relief from the handwriting testimony, Proponent from time to time read into the record testimony of various individuals taken at pre-trial depositions. Two of these were prominent medical experts from the East and Midwest specializing in diseases of the kidney, an ailment contributing to Hughes's death. Neither one of the doctors had treated Hughes during his lifetime, but from past medical records testified as to the progress and severity of his kidney disease. Proponent's attorney Rhoden then led both medical experts down the primrose path of attributing the illiterate, clumsy appearance of the Mormon will writing to Hughes's kidney failure. On being shown a copy of the will, one doctor stated that the misspellings, overwrites, and decrepit nature of the script were consistent with the effect on the brain of renal failure. The other stated that he could detect signs of kidney disorder in the Mormon will by such things as "deletions of letters, faulty punctuation, oversimplification of thoughts, simple sentences—all consistent with the effect on the brain of renal failure." One example he cited was leaving the *h* out of the word children.

I do not know how much credence the jury gave this medical testimony, but one thing was quite apparent—both experts had expressed opinions based solely on inspection of the Mormon will writings without recourse to Hughes's known specimens. I wondered if they would have changed their opinions had they been shown that memo I saw in Jack Harris's office of Hughes's fluent, literate, and skillfully composed writing dated just one day before March 19th of 1968, the date affixed to the Mormon will.

Arnold Etman of Holland was the last of Proponent's handwriting experts to take the witness stand. Short, plump, and balding, Etman was a man I judged to be in his sixties. His expressive face was framed by sideburns and a well-trimmed goatee. When he spoke, the words were carefully chosen and delivered in letter-perfect English. I could tell from the way Proponent's attorney respectfully led Arnold Etman to the witness stand and guided him through his seemingly impressive qualifications that they were counting on him to be their savior. At this point they definitely needed one.

One of the roles I play as a questioned document examiner is to provide my own attorney with suggested cross-examination questions for the opposing experts. I have always felt that this kind of assistance is perfectly proper when the opposing expert is testifying against the facts and making statements that are scientifically unverifiable or perhaps untruthful. There may be no other sources of information available to the attorneys, especially when the expert is from some foreign country.

During the pre-trial stages of the Hughes case, Jack Harris and I contacted several European forensic document examiners with whom we were acquainted to find out what they knew about Etman, Faideau, and Ollivier. No additional information was needed about the sole American expert. Other than hearsay remarks about the reputations of the three Europeans, we obtained very little hard evidence relating to their backgrounds. It was particularly difficult to find out anything about Arnold Etman except that he may have made some mistakes when he was document examiner for the Ministry of Justice between 1955 and 1975, at which time he retired.

Had we been able to secure information on Etman's post-war years, we would have learned that he spent several years in a Dutch prison after being convicted of Nazi collaboration. Whether this information would have had any effect upon a jury is doubtful, although it might have tarnished some of Etman's cultivated, well-polished image.

Etman's use of English was as long-winded as it was impeccable. He testified on direct examination for an unbelievable nine full days about every jot and tittle in the Mormon will writing *except* that pointing to forgery. He used ruled graphs designed for graphological studies and transparency films of the handwriting, but mostly he stood in front of the jury lecturing—like—like a Dutch school master. I dozed off from time to time and could see that the jury was doing likewise.

As Etman's testimony on direct examination was about to end, the mood of the courtroom was suddenly changed by an incident that could have only happened in this unbelievable trial. Following an afternoon recess, Judge Hayes asked Harold Rhoden and Contestants' attorneys to approach the bench. "Gentlemen," he said, "I have just received in the mail another holographic will, purportedly written by Howard Hughes, which I think should be brought to your attention." The judge continued, "Ordinarily, I would have thrown this document in the waste basket, as I have many others, except that this one bears a most interesting return address on the envelope." Pausing dramatically, Judge Hayes pointed to Proponent's lawyer Harold Rhoden and said, "The name on the return address is yours, Mr. Rhoden, and the address is your Beverly Hills office in Los Angeles."

I developed a grudging admiration for Harold Rhoden during the course of the trial. He was able to shrug off the most damaging of testimony and plow on to some new crisis. But this document sent to Judge Hayes impugned his name and reputation. "Judge," he stammered as he excitedly marched up and down in front of the judge's bench, "I know nothing about this will." Casting a suspicious eye towards Contestants' attorneys, "Somebody must be playing a dirty trick on me." Rhoden finally became so agitated that the judge called a recess for him to regain his composure.

Jack Harris and I both examined this new "will" which was almost identical in content to the Mormon will except for a change from the Boy Scouts of America to the Girl Scouts. Both of us agreed that it was a better forgery than the Mormon will. Even so, Proponent's experts solemnly declared that examination had revealed unexplainable differences they had not found in the Mormon will writing that definitely pointed to forgery. The reference to the Mormon will comparison seemed absurd to us but at least all of the experts could finally agree on something—the "Rhoden will" was a "rank forgery." The judge discounted the entire affair as being someone's attempt to poke fun at the Mormon will.

Court reconvened the next morning for Contestants' cross-examination of Etman to which I contributed in no small measure. After two days of questioning and evasive responses, everyone in the courtroom except Etman was completely exhausted. In answer to Rhoden's final question on redirect, "Is it possible for it [the Mormon will] to be a forgery?" Etman responded indignantly, "No, of course not."

I was the last handwriting witness to testify in the case. I had been preceded by Proponent's three European experts and one American; two more, Harris and Shaneyfelt testifying for Contestants; plus deposition testimony from a number of others read into the record. The opinions reached by the latter group were not to Harold Rhoden's liking, and he obviously found it far better to have their testimony read to the jury than to have them appear in person to explain why the Mormon will was such an obvious forgery.

"Contestants call Donald Doud to the witness stand," announced attorney Dilworth. How many times have I heard these words during my half-century career as a forensic document examiner—well over five hundred! And each time I do there is that familiar queasy feeling in the pit of the stomach and flush of excitement that actors and athletes are said to experience before appearing on stage or in some competition. All nervousness soon disappears in the heat of the battle.

As I placed my hand on the *Bible*, swearing "to tell the truth, the whole truth, and nothing but the truth," I glanced over at the table reserved for Contestants' attorneys. All three were smiling smugly in the belief that their last handwriting witness was about to explode a series of unexpected bombshells that would blow Proponent's case out of the water. They were particularly gleeful about one final bit of pyrotechnics reserved for the very end of my testimony.

Some eighteen months after the conclusion of the Mormon will trial, Harold Rhoden wrote a book titled *High Stakes*[1]—a chapter titled "The Rapier" being devoted to the testimony of "Edwin Arledge," a pseudonym given me for some unknown reason. The first paragraph is particularly revealing of the way some lawyers view expert witnesses—not by the content of their testimony but by the effect of that testimony upon the jury:

> Earl Yokum [attorney James Dilworth] called the last of Contestants' handwriting experts, Edwin Arledge of Chicago. Tall, grandfatherly Edwin Arledge smiled when his name was called, and seemed to be a likeable and gentle man. As Sam Mayerson watched Arledge walk to the witness stand, he whispered, 'Be careful with this guy, the jurors are going to love him.'

Love me or not, it was quite plain that after seven months of trial the jurors were going to be quite impatient if I spent more time

---

1. Harold Rhoden, *High Stakes: The Gamble for the Howard Hughes Will* (New York: Crown, 1980).

than was absolutely necessary on my presentation. From the testimony of experts on both sides, they had learned all they wanted to about letter form similarities and differences, misspellings, tremor in the strokes, writing anachronisms and pen lifts. About the only relief from the tedium was provided by Jack Harris, who had a knack for keeping the jury interested through the use of colorful metaphors and a wry sense of humor. His last comparison exhibit was a classic example. He hung the mural-size exhibit in front of the jury with no comment—and waited. Then, one by one, the jurors started to chuckle and guffaw as they grasped the significance of the words Jack had chosen to compare: "This is not my will HRH." Even Proponent's attorney Harold Rhoden had to laugh at that one.

But now it was my turn. As I switched on my overhead projector and told the jury that I intended to concentrate my testimony primarily on evidence connecting the Mormon will forgery with published sources of Hughes's writing, I could sense by the way they leaned forward in their seats that they were going to be most interested in what I had to say. In the backs of their minds, I am sure, was a vital question that needed to be answered: Where would a potential forger of the Mormon will find specimens of the reclusive Howard Hughes's writing to copy, and how could that connection be established? I was there to supply the answer with demonstrative exhibits as simple and understandable as I could make them. Summarized and condensed from over one hundred pages of trial transcripts is what I told the jury:

The one page "C and B" reprint in the book *Hoax* contained, from an alphabetical standpoint, thirteen different capitals, as did the two-page reprint of that same document in *Life*. The Mormon will and envelope contained twenty-two, a difference of nine. These nine capitals formed the principal basis for my findings that the Howard Hughes writings in "C and B" were used as the copying source for the Mormon will forgeries. Every one of the nine differed fundamentally from Hughes's writing habits, whereas the other thirteen were crude but obvious imitations of the "C and B" capitals.

I then flashed on the screen examples of the *J, F, V, K, W, S, U, E,* and *O* from Hughes's genuine writing as compared to the same capitals from the Mormon will. The differences were so dramatic as to need little elaboration. I glanced over at the jury and could tell from their nodding heads that they felt the same. I placed special emphasis on four of those capitals, the *J, P, V,* and *K*. They were the strangest looking letters of all. Not only did they differ fundamentally from Hughes's writing, but they didn't look like any system of writing ever taught in the United States or anywhere else for that matter. The explanation for these oddities, I told the jury, rested within the mind of the forger, who decided upon a very dangerous solution for the problem of the missing capitals. He decided to enlarge *small* letters from the "C and B" reprint to the size of capitals. How was he to know that Hughes's capital forms were so totally different from his small letters. The appearance of the enlarged *k* was absolutely ridiculous.

I next took up the subject of the Howard R. Hughes signatures appearing at the bottom of all three pages of the will and on the envelope, illustrating my remarks with a series of comparison exhibits. The evidence is strong, I told the jury, that all four were

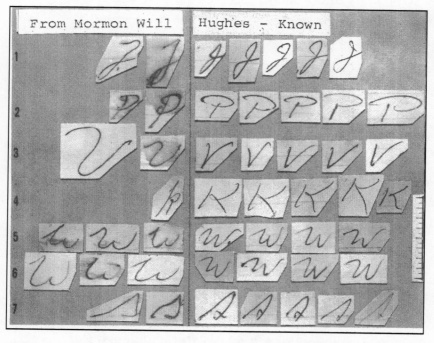

Hughes's habits of making the *J*, *P*, and *K* as shown on the right side of the chart were completely violated in the questioned will. Capitals at the left were missing from the C & B letter, used as the forger's exemplar of Hughes's writing, so the forger resorted to the ridiculous alternative of enlarging the small letters of the C & B to the size of capitals.

written in attempted imitation of Howard R. Hughes's reproduced signatures appearing in the centerfold section of *Hoax*. I reached that conclusion for the following reasons:

The reduced size "interrogatory signatures" in *Hoax* both contained gaps at the left side of the *R* as did all four signatures on the Mormon will. Not one of the over eighty genuine signatures of Howard R. Hughes I examined had a similar gap in the *R*, nor did the *originals* of the interrogatory signatures themselves. So, why this curious discrepancy in the reproduced signatures? The answer lies with the printing process used for the *Hoax* reproductions, the images of which are made up of tiny dots arranged in accordance with the light and dark areas of the original signatures. The process failed to record the faint left side of Hughes's *R* caused by his habit of releasing the pressure on the pen at that point. The forger of the Mormon will signatures made the fatal mistake of copying this deficiency in the printing process into his attempted imitations.

I concluded my testimony on direct examination with the last of the "pyrotechnics" promised by Contestants' attorneys. This had to do with the first line of the will and my conclusion that the name "Howard" and the initial *R* in "I Howard R. Hughes being of..." were *traced* from the second interrogatory signature in *Hoax*. This was a different kind of evidence than my earlier testimony about the missing left side of the *R's*. A tracing attempt established a *physical connection* between the Mormon will forgery and the signature from *Hoax*. That, coupled with the missing centerfold section from the Weber State copy of *Hoax* with Dummar's fingerprint on it, would have established Melvin's modus operandi—at least that's what Contestants' attorneys believed. I was more interested in trying to demonstrate before a very tired jury the logic of my conviction that the forger of the Mormon will tried to trace the first Howard R. Hughes name on the will. My explanation to the jury was as follows.

The interrogatory signature in *Hoax* used as the model for the tracing was reduced in size by about one-third, making the "Howard R" portion smaller than all but one of the eighty known signatures of Hughes I had examined. The "Hughes" part of the name was normal in size.

Using transparency films, I then superimposed the interrogatory signature over the "Howard" portion of the questioned signature. They matched almost perfectly in letter forms, length, height, and spacing between the letters. There was an unnatural sameness to the two, and equally important, they were both diminutive in size. The *R's* also superimposed closely, but there was a slight difference in the relationship of the *R* to the name "Howard." The hand is not like a printing press, I told the jury, and slight differences of this kind are to be expected due to a shifting of the paper during the tracing process. I also pointed out another connecting link—the gap in the left side of the *R* similar to that present in the four signatures to the will and envelope.

Is it just a coincidence, I asked the jury, that the "Howard R." in the will matches up almost perfectly in size and letter forms with that tiny signature in *Hoax*, even to the printing flaw at the left side of the *R*? I think not. It is far more reasonable to believe that the forger started to trace the name from the *Hoax* example and, realizing the difficulty of following such a small, faint image, abandoned the effort after the *R*.

A third, and more subjective, area that I didn't discuss with the jury involved the location of the diminutive "Howard R" combination on the first line of the Mormon will. This, in turn, suggested a logical scenario in which the forger first attempted to copy Howard Hughes's signature the easy way, by tracing. Then, realizing the difficulties of executing this type of forgery on a wide-scale basis, he abandoned the effort at midpoint and forged the rest of the will by free-hand imitation. Logical? Yes, but it was something I would have to leave to the attorneys to argue.

The tracing evidence concluded my testimony on direct examination. It had consumed less than two hours of time that hot afternoon in May 1978, and now I was being turned over to the Proponent's attorney, Harold Rhoden, for cross-examination. As I glanced over in his direction, I could see that this normally unflappable man seemed to be in a highly agitated state. The final bit of "pyrotechnics" Contestants' attorneys had promised seemed to have diminished Rhoden's confidence in the legitimacy of the Mormon will. In his book *High Stakes*, Rhoden writes of his reaction to my testimony:

> Could it be a tracing? My God, could I have been wrong about the whole case? About the evidence that made a forgery impossible, about the ink (the evidence

of its manufacturing date was uncertain) and the medical evidence and the handwriting, about the evidence that Forsythe could not have made up this story about knowing Hughes. No, it couldn't possibly be a tracing. Could it? No!

With his composure apparently restored, Rhoden came back into the courtroom after a brief recess to conduct what I thought would be a two or three day cross-examination on the three points of my testimony to which I had devoted most of my time. He had cross-examined Jack Harris for two days and Lyndal Shaneyfelt for almost a week, and I could see no good reason why he wouldn't do the same with me. But to my surprise, the sole source of Rhoden's concern seemed to be the tracing evidence about which I alone had testified. Using a large sheet of paper tacked onto a board, Rhoden drew in large red letters "Howard R" as it purportedly appeared in the Mormon will. Then, using a blue crayon, he superimposed a drawing of the signature from *Hoax*, which, to no one's surprise, varied dramatically from the red line. I don't often lose my temper on the witness stand, but I objected strenuously to being cross-examined about Rhoden's self-serving drawings when the original transparency films I had used on direct examination were available for the same purpose. Judge Hayes didn't agree with my objections and told me not to argue with counsel.

For the better part of the afternoon, Rhoden hammered away at the slight differences between the will and *Hoax* examples of "Howard R," differences that were greatly exaggerated in the huge drawing the judge permitted him to use. My answer was always the same. Unlike a rubber stamp or printed impression, human actions, including handwriting, are always subject to some variability even when attempting to trace from some genuine signature. Tracing from a very small signature compounds the difficulty, and perhaps that was one of the reasons why the tracing attempt was discontinued at midpoint.

To my surprise, Rhoden's cross-examination included some of the same subjective reasoning about which I was reluctant to testify on direct examination. For example, in one question Rhoden asked:

Q: Why do you suppose that a forger would have traced only the writing on line one—and not even the last name—and not any of the other three signatures in the will or the signature on the envelope or the other three hundred words in the will?

A: When the tracing didn't work well on line one, he decided to use the free hand method for the rest.

Q: You mean, he decided not to continue tracing because the tracing was not a good tracing?

A: Ask the forger!

To everyone's relief, including the jury's, Rhoden had just one final question to ask me, and I had anticipated what it would be.

Proponent had searched through a large number of Howard Hughes signatures looking for the unusual, as they did earlier with 450 pages of cursive writings—trying to reconcile the size difference. I had examined eighty of Hughes's signatures on promissory notes and had found only one example where the "Howard R." was about the same size as the *Hoax* signature. In *High Stakes* Rhoden tells of cross-examining me on that point, again using my pseudonym, "Edwin Arledge":

> Mr. Arledge, you said that one reason that you found the will to be a forgery was that the writing in this [the 'Howard R'] was smaller than the writings from Mr. Hughes's exemplars. If I were to show you writings from Mr. Hughes's exemplars that were smaller — smaller in letters and in words — than the writing in the will, would you be willing to admit as to just this one factor, that it was not significant?

> I would not.

> I have no further questions.

I was astonished that Rhoden would quit without showing to the jury the one signature out of eighty where the "Howard R" was as small as the *Hoax* example. I was even more astonished when he abruptly terminated my cross-examination. Whether he was afraid of my answers or of boring the jury further I do not know. From my own standpoint, after a year and one-half of stressful participation in this frustrating and bizarre case, I was grateful to be finally done with the whole business.

In the airport on my way back to Milwaukee I picked up a copy of the *Las Vegas Sun*. The headline about my tracing evidence read: "BOMBSHELL EVIDENCE EXPLODES IN HUGHES WILL TRIAL." The morning headline in the *Review Journal* read: 'MORMON WILL TRACED."

Two days later, on May 4, 1978, attorneys for the Contestants rested. Harold Rhoden offered no witnesses to rebut my testimony or that of any other witness, and the evidence portion of the case ground to a halt.

"Proponent rests," shouted Harold Rhoden with unexpected brevity. But he and the attorneys for Contestants were still not finished. Closing arguments consumed another eight days of time and probably did more harm than good. The jury was obviously irritated, having been told initially that the case would be over in a matter of weeks, only to find themselves in the seventh month of trial, forced to listen to eight more days of histrionics. Judge Hayes didn't seem to be bothered at all and, from all reports, basked in the light of spectator and media attention to the end.

After seven months of scientific and unscientific testimony, legal high-jinks, bizarre witnesses, and unusual judicial behavior, the trial to determine the status of the "most examined will in history" finally went to the jury.

On June 8, 1978, after elevem hours of deliberation, the jury came out with their verdict: "We, the jury, find that the purported three page will dated March 19, 1968 *was not written by Howard R. Hughes*."

Following the verdict, one of Contestants' attorneys conducted a jury polling to determine which of the handwriting witnesses was the most impressive. To everyone's surprise, Arnold Etman of Holland, who I would agree was a charming fellow, was near the top of the list, even though the jury felt he was dead wrong in his opinion. This same dichotomy of values is found in the political arena today where sound bites are more important than substance.

Insofar as my tracing evidence was concerned, the jury was not convinced—at least it wasn't as important to them in reaching a verdict as the other evidence. Unquestionably, this was the most difficult of all my points to explain, and perhaps I hadn't done a good job of it. Or perhaps the jury was just too bored and disgruntled to absorb anything new requiring a different kind of reasoning.

At least I can find some consolation in Harold Rhoden's words from *High Stakes*. He considered my tracing evidence to be the most devastating of all, as did his assistant Linda who was quoted as saying, "I sat there in the courtroom today, and if I had to cast a vote right now, and if I were going to be honest, I'd have to vote that it's a forgery." But whether or not the jury believed my forgery-by-tracing testimony was really irrelevant, they were totally convinced by the additional points of evidence branding the Mormon will a forgery.

As an epilogue to the trial, Melvin Dummar, who for various reasons could not be identified as the writer of the Mormon will and who perjured himself on numerous occasions (but never under oath) went Scot free. To make matters worse, Dummar ended up making a small fortune playing in country music bands around the country. (Whether or not "Santa's Souped Up Sleigh" was part of his repertoire I do not know.)

Harold Rhoden, cagey attorney for Proponent, went back to Los Angeles after the trial to work for palimony lawyer Marvin Mitchelson, co-counsel during parts of the Mormon will trial, to whom he was deeply in debt. After several years of servitude to Mitchelson, Rhoden, who had been a flyer since World War II, made enough money to again afford his own plane. I am told that he and his family were killed shortly thereafter while flying in inclement weather.

Judge Keith Hayes also suffered a premature, but more predictable, death from cancer. In the Epilogue to *High Stakes,* Rhoden tells about a deathbed visit made by a friend to the hospital room of Judge Hayes, who was asked to name the two souls he would most look forward to greeting in the next world. "Keith said the first was his mother—then *Howard Hughes.* Keith said something about a question he wanted to ask him." While his Mormon religion may have blinded Judge Hayes to the truth, I suspect that Harold Rhoden knew the answer all along.

In his own hereafter, Rhoden might not have been surprised to hear Howard Hughes affirm the words on Jack Harris's comparison exhibit: "This is not my will. HRH." But, he would have cross-examined Hughes nevertheless—long into eternity.

7

From Daniel to Digital: A Little Bit of History

Questioned document examiners, or forensic document examiners as we are commonly known today, trace our roots to the old handwriting experts of ancient times, most of whom were translators of foreign scripts. Daniel of the *Bible* may have been one of the first, but his prophetic translation of the mysterious writing on the wall offended King Nebuchadenezzar, and he ended up in the lion's den for his honesty.

Historical records abound with other early examples of handwriting experts translating Aramaic, Egyptian, Roman, and Greek documents, and in some cases examining the script for authenticity. In those days, strange as it may seem, forgery of handwriting (and art works) was considered to be more of a compliment to the victim than a crime. Depending on the quality of the imitation, punishment of the culprit could range all the way from a mild rebuke for a skilled imitation to a public lashing for a bad one. This laissez-faire attitude towards unauthorized copying pretty much ended during the middle ages when land titles and "bills of hand" became the objects of wholesale forgery for which the perpetrators usually suffered the death penalty. Yet, even the prospect of death did not deter ninety-four thousand English citizens from forging an issue of one pound notes (temptingly written in pen and ink on white paper). Seventy-seven hundred of the offenders were executed.

In 1548, a year after the death of King Henry VIII, followers of Mary Queen of Scots employed a handwriting expert to examine the signatures on Henry's last will and testament—a document that conspicuously failed to mention the beheaded queen's Stuart line of descendancy to the English throne. There is no historical record of what the expert found. Four hundred twenty years later I examined the same signatures of Henry VIII and reached a rather surprising conclusion—a conclusion that might have changed the course of history had it been the subject of serious legal dispute in the days following Henry's death.

Throughout the years, handwriting experts have figured prominently in other disputes involving the writing of famous or, in some cases, infamous people. For years, the authorship of William Shakespeare's plays has been a contentious issue among historians, many believing that the actor "William Shakespeare," from Stratford on Avon, was too ignorant to have penned the beautiful works. Unfortunately, the original handwritten drafts for *Hamlet* and the other great Shakespearean plays were either destroyed or lost, leaving only one handwritten scene from the play

Sir Thomas More (to which several playwrights contributed) as a possible source of his fertile pen. But according to prominent document experts from England and America, the draft of this scene differed substantially from the oddly spelled but unquestionably genuine signature "William Shakespeare" on his will. So the debate goes on.

At the turn of the century, an itinerant lawyer by the name of Albert Patrick was convicted of forging the will of William Marsh Rice, founder of the Rice Institute in Houston, Texas, and of plotting for the old man's murder. Sensational accounts of the handwriting testimony flashed across the pages of the nation's newspapers, including that of a feisty little man who later became my Milwaukee associate. Some time later the nation's attention was riveted on the handwriting evidence that helped convict Al Capone of income tax evasion, and on the testimony of eight handwriting experts at the Hauptmann-Lindbergh trial, all of whom agreed that Hauptmann wrote the ransom notes.

During the late nineteenth century and well into the twentieth, less than twenty American handwriting experts were qualified to examine cases of suspected forgery. While a few of them came out of criminological or other backgrounds, most were former teachers of penmanship at business colleges. In those days, students were required to write legible, attractive script as a prerequisite for graduation. The teaching of handwriting also taught the teachers, in the best way possible, to recognize signs of both genuineness and forgery in disputed handwriting.

Those early pioneers were innovative, intelligent, energetic, opinionated, and sometimes eccentric men. I should know—I trained under three of the greatest[1] of them. They had to design their own equipment for measuring, comparing, and photographing handwriting. They had to devise standardized procedures for their examinations. They had to fight a constant battle with the legal community to achieve acceptance of expert testimony in court, and they had to cling together for support, education, and survival.

Starting in 1910, the profession took a dramatic leap into the modern era when Albert S. Osborn of New York published his first book, *Questioned Documents*,[2] and in the process established a new title, "questioned document examiners," for those who examined disputed documents. This was a much more descriptive and inclusive term than "handwriting experts" and served to embrace a diversity of new problems sparked by products of the industrial revolution. In common use now were typewriters, adding machines, facsimile devices, automated machines for making watermarked papers, different kinds of adhesives, rubber stamps, fountain pens, and inks. The questioned document examiner was forced to expand his areas of expertise accordingly.

Osborn emphasized that an expert's opinion was no better than the reasons given for it and advocated laws to remove archaic legal

---

1. Albert D. Osborn, Clark Sellers, H. J. Walter.

2. Albert Sherman Osborn, *Questioned Documents: A Study of Questioned Documents with an Outline of Methods by Which the Fact May be Discovered and Shown* (Rochester, NY: The Lawyers' Co-operative Publishing Co., 1910).

restrictions on the introduction of comparison writings and use of demonstrative evidence in court. The legal community was at first reluctant to accept this radical new approach to expert testimony; but as time went on, their objections fell by the wayside, first in federal and finally in state courts. The legal chains of the past were coming unshackled, and examiners of questioned documents now had the resources to examine evidence scientifically and to effectively demonstrate their findings.

In those early days, questioned document experts in private practice or in privately run laboratories handled both civil and virtually all criminal cases for federal, state, county, and local units of government. This all changed in 1929 at the time of Al Capone's St. Valentine's Day massacre in Chicago when Northwestern University established the nation's first crime detection laboratory to help law enforcement personnel track down the killers through scientific study of the bullets and other evidence left at the crime scene.

The success of Northwestern University's crime laboratory sparked a revolution of sorts throughout the country with similar laboratories being established by virtually all branches of government including the FBI, post office department, Secret Service, IRS, the military, and various regional and local units. Civil cases and criminal defense cases became the realms of the private questioned document expert.

Today the numbers of forensic document examiners in both the public and private sectors have grown spectacularly. So, too, have the diverse types of cases submitted for their examination: altered medical records in malpractice lawsuits, photocopy forgeries, computer frauds using word processing equipment, sophisticated methods of aging documents, mechanical forgery of signatures, and color copying of currency, among others.

New technologies for solving these crimes have also developed rapidly. Computer-enhanced images in the infrared and ultraviolet enable examiners to decipher erased writings and to compare inks and papers for color and composition. Ink chemists are approaching the point where they can determine the relative ages of inks by sophisticated testing procedures. Digital technologies are being used for instant photography and for expediting research into subjects such as handwriting, typewriting, computers, and copiers. Electrostatic equipment (ESDA) is now available to provide greatly enhanced images of indentations in paper created by one document being written on top of another or by some other means.

I would have given my right arm for ESDA technology in 1966 when I was called to examine the last will of King Henry VIII, and conducted a fruitless search for evidence of indentations next to the king's signature.

8

A Ghostly Royal Hand:
The Mysterious Last Will and
Testament of King Henry VIII

Vain the ambitions of Kings
Who seek by trophies and dead things
to leave a living name behind
And weave but nets to catch the wind

JOHN WEBSTER, *The Devil's Law Case*

After months of frustrating delays, I was finally in the Public Record Office, London, about to examine the last will and testament of King Henry VIII. As Dr. Latham, Assistant Keeper of Historical Records, ushered me into the small room that was to be my workplace for the next three days, I could almost hear the raucous voice of that "Serene and Invincible Prince" screaming in protest, "Knave, what are you doing with my last will and testament? The legality of that document was established 420 years ago when the Stuart descendants of that scheming woman, Mary

Queen of Scots, failed in their attempt to overthrow my will. Executioner, off with this man's head!"

Knowing that my head was probably safe from dismemberment, I might have reminded the king of the final days of his life and the fruitless efforts by members of his privy chamber to persuade him to sign the will that had been awaiting his signature for many weeks. I might even have suggested the possibility that his stubborn refusal to sign the will was deliberate—a means of keeping his ambitious counselors at bay until the last moment. "It was because of your foolhardy scheme," I would have told him, "that I am now in the Public Record Office trying to settle a dispute about whether or not you *ever* got around to signing your own will."

The date was December 30, 1546. King Henry VIII had exactly one month of life remaining to impose that dominating and inflexible will on his English subjects. Suffering from a variety of illnesses including inflamed varicose ulcers, recurring symptoms of syphilis, an irregular heartbeat that

Henry VIII.

caused frequent spells of dizziness, and "urine of dropsy," a disease that puffed his body up to grotesque proportions, Henry was able to move about only with great difficulty. Indeed, when it became necessary for him to leave his bedchamber, four men were required to carry his huge body about the palace in a specially reinforced litter. Yet the royal monarch was still a commanding and intimidating figure, shouting orders and chastising those who had the misfortune to cross him.

Four days earlier on December 26, 1546, a scrivener trained in the art of handwriting had drafted Henry's last will and testament. Apparently presented to the king with great formality, the fourteen-page document was essentially a revision of a 1544 will and was dated, according to Henry's instructions, December 30, 1546. Presumably Henry meant to sign it on that same day, but the historical evidence is strong that he did not. For his own reasons, Henry postponed to some future time the signing of this most important instrument for disposing of his assets, rewarding the faithful, and transferring power (or as some would have it, ruling from the grave). Indeed, William Clerk, a member of the Privy Council and one of Henry's aides, received a tongue-lashing from the royal monarch for trying to pressure him to sign the will without further delay.

The contents of the will, written in old English script, were as remarkable as the person who conceived them. Surprisingly Catholic in tone, the will not only disposed of Henry's possessions and rewarded his faithful councilors with less than generous annuities and land grants, but more importantly, made provisions of his line of succession, which inexplicably violated the traditional line of blood descendancy. After first naming his ten-year-old son Edward to succeed him followed by daughters Mary and Elizabeth and providing for the establishment of a Council of Regency to govern during his son's minority, the line of succession then jumped to the Suffolk descendants of his younger sister Mary rather than the Stuart descendants of Margaret, his older sister. This was a blunder that was to cause much friction and ill feelings in the days following Henry's death.

History records that the will remained unsigned throughout most of the month of January 1547 until the 27th, when Henry's health condition dramatically worsened. Now completely bedridden and drifting in and out of consciousness, it was obvious to all that he had only a brief time left to live. History further records that on the afternoon of that fateful day, the will was delivered to his bedchambers, again by William Clerk, who must have been frantic at this point, knowing that the document was still unsigned. Did Henry himself request delivery of the will? History is mute on the subject.

During the remainder of the late afternoon and early evening of January 27, 1547, the will remained unsigned. Some historians believe that this was due to sheer obstinacy on Henry's part or, more likely, a way of holding a Damocles sword over the heads of his ambitious councilors, many of whom were already engaged in a behind-the-scenes struggle for power. Others disagree, holding that Henry did not sign his will because he simply did not have the physical or mental ability to do so.

From about 8:30 PM the night of January 27th until the time of his death at two o'clock on the morning of January 28, 1547, an iron curtain appears to have been drawn around the bedchamber of the ailing king. History only records that Henry's physical condition deteriorated suddenly and dramatically until he lapsed into unconsciousness and finally death. What final acts he was able to perform during these six fateful hours nobody knows. In the days following Henry's death, those who were present in that closed bedchamber, including his councilors, members of the privy chamber, physicians, and a musician sent to make Henry's last hours "more pleasant," were curiously silent about the events of that night, and perhaps for good reason.

As to the will itself, it again surfaced sometime during the daylight hours of January 28, 1547, bearing the signatures of Henry VIII on the first and last pages and the signatures of *eleven* members of his privy chamber as witnesses to the alleged signing. The final words on page fourteen read: *"signed by my most gracious hand,"* followed by the signature *"Henry R" (Rex)*.

With the foregoing scenario, could there be any question that, somehow or other during those six fateful hours, Henry VIII was able to gather his mental and physical powers sufficiently to sign his name to the first and last pages of the will? As I was destined to learn, there was indeed a serious question, and I was to be the focal point of efforts to resolve it.

I first became involved in this unusual historical problem in 1964 when Dr. Lacey Baldwin Smith, Professor of English Literature at Northwestern University contacted me with an unusual assignment. A noted authority on the life of King Henry VIII, Professor Smith asked me to help settle a heated dispute taking place between himself and a fellow historian, Professor Mortimer Levine of West Virginia University.

It all started with an article[1] written by Dr. Smith for *The Journal of British Studies* titled, "The Last Will and Testament of Henry VIII: A Question of Perspective." This article challenged many of the past theories of a group of historians known as the "traditionalists," including their belief that Henry's last will and testament was signed on the first and last pages by the king himself and on the date indicated—December 30, 1546. Dr. Smith believed just the opposite—that the signatures were not handwritten by Henry but, in fact, may have been placed there by a *dry stamp* device shortly before or after the king's death.

In further support of his theory, Smith described a Registry of Stamped Documents, "Which the King's Majesty caused me, William Clerk, to stamp with his Highness's secret stamp, at diverse times and places during the month of January (1547)." Henry's will was number 85, and next to last on the list. The final entry, number 86, was the attainder (death sentence) for the Duke

---

1. Lacey Baldwin Smith, "The Last Will and Testament of Henry VIII: A Question of Perspective", *The Journal of British Studies*, Vol 2, No. 1 (November 1962), pp. 14-27.

A Ghostly Royal Hand
The Mysterious Last Will and Testament of Henry VIII

of Norfolk, one of Henry's trusted aides. He apparently got too cozy with Mary Queen of Scots and was sentenced to lose his head for the dalliance. Unlike other entries on the page, neither 85 nor 86 was initialed by the king.

Responding to Dr. Smith's article, Professor Mortimer Levine of West Virginia University wrote in *The Historian*[1] that he had seen the two signatures on the will and the strokes varied enough to convince him they were genuinely handwritten by King Henry VIII. Moreover, it seemed highly unlikely that eleven members of his privy counsel would have signed their names as witnesses if they hadn't actually seen Henry sign his will. As to the date of signing, many historical accounts of that event were erroneous or based upon hearsay.

Was the listing of Henry's will in the register a mistake, as Dr. Levine and other traditionalists suggest? Or perhaps the illegality of a stamped will was suggested after the document was entered in the register and another will hastily drawn up and signed by the king's own hand. Would King Henry VIII have authorized the use of a stamp for the most important document of his lifetime and thereby run the risk of legal challenges from followers of Mary Queen of Scots or of other enemies from within?

As for the dry stamp itself, Dr. Smith explained that it was a device used by King Henry (and other royalty of the past) for the

---

1. Mortimer Levine, "The Last Will and Testament or Henry VIII: A Reappraisal Appraised", *Historian* 26 (1964): 471-85.

Ihesus

In the name of god and of the glorious and blessed
virgin our Lady Saint Mary and of all the holy
company of Heaven We Henry by the grace
of god king of England France and Ireland
defender of the faith and in earth immediately
under god the Supreme head of the church of
England and Ireland of that name the eight
calling to our remembrance the great gifts and
benefits of Almighty god given unto us in this
transitory life gyven unto him our most hearty
and humble thanks knowledging ourselves insufficient
in any part to deserve or recompense the same
But fear that we have not worthely receyved
the same And considering further also in ourselves
that we be as all mankind is mortall and born
in synne believing neverthelesse and hoping that every
christen creature lyving here in this transitory and
wretched world under god dying in stedfast
and perfait faith endeavoring and exercising himself
to execute in his lief tyme if he have leasure such
good deeds and charitable works as scripture commandeth
and as may be to the honour and pleasure of god

Page 1 of Henry VIII will. Note signature at the top.

Last page of Henry VIII will. Note signature toward the center of the page.

signing of both routine documents such as correspondence and passports, and, occasionally, for more important documents such as letters patent (royal directives). Much like the autopen signatures of presidents today, it was intended to save the royal monarch the inconvenience of having to sign documents in person.

Little is known about the precise makeup of Henry's dry stamp device, said Dr. Smith, because it was highly protected during his lifetime and immediately destroyed after his death. Based upon the technology available at that time, it seems likely that the basic unit was composed of soft metal upon which was cast or carved a raised mirror outline of the king's signature. By means of some kind of pressure mechanism, perhaps similar to the modern notary seal having both positive and negative jaws, one of three councilors, usually William Clerk, would impress a grooved outline of the king's signature into the surface of the paper.

The same councilor would then direct a low light source, perhaps from a candle or lantern, across the surface of the document so that the grooves could be seen and filled in with pen and ink. The other two councilors were required by royal decree to be present during the entire process.

As an interesting sidelight to the use of this stamp, King Henry VIII apparently recognized that signatures thus executed were tantamount to forgeries and regularly pardoned his councilors "of all treasons concerning the counterfeiting, impression and writing of the King's sign manual."

Despite these reassuring words, it was apparent that many of the king's entourage including Clerk and another councilor, Sir

William Paget who also impressed the king's "sign manual" on documents, were concerned about their own culpability. Indeed, sometime *after* Henry's death, Paget and Clerk gave their support to young Edward's annulment of Norfolk's sentence based upon the stamped signature on the attainder. This apparently failed, and poor Norfolk eventually lost his head to a less forgiving Queen Elizabeth. William Clerk, the stamp's custodian, may have been worried about losing his cranium for another reason. He sought a pardon from Elizabeth for the "mechanical forging" of her father's signature.

It was now 1966, and my wife and I had just arrived in London after a brief morning flight from Copenhagen where I had given a talk before the document section of the International Association of Forensic Sciences. Speaking to 250 colleagues from all over the world proved to be a memorable experience, but it was nothing compared to the prospect of examining a document 420 years old purportedly signed by that most contentious and colorful of all British rulers, King Henry VIII. What a story I would be able to tell my children and grandchildren about this unique experience!

It was only a short taxi ride from the Strand Hotel to the Public Record Office, which, I had been told, contained not only the royal wills from the beginning of British history but all of the treaties, grants, commissions, and other historical documents relating to Britain's great past. "There she be, govanah—the house of history," barked my Cockney cabby as we drew up to a dingy, unimpressive-looking greystone building. As I finally found the

193

right coins to pay the fare, I could not help but notice a much more imposing structure next door identified as the Royal Courts of Justice where, I was told, many of Henry VIII's subjects, including two of his wives, were sentenced to death.

With a letter of introduction in hand from Dr. Lacey Baldwin Smith, I somewhat timidly entered the door of the Public Record Office. Being cautious, as most Americans are, of British pride in their history, and knowing that this research concerned the rather sacrosanct institution of British royalty, it was with some uneasiness that I presented my letter of introduction to the receptionist, who in turn delivered it to a small, adjoining office. In a few seconds, out bounded an exuberant, slender, somewhat balding figure who immediately came over and grasped my hand and said, "My name is Dr. Latham and I am Assistant Keeper of Historical Records. We have heard that you were coming. My staff and I will do everything possible to make your research efforts here pleasant. Please call on us if there is anything you need." When invited to have afternoon tea with him and his staff, I was elated and almost launched into a recital of my Guilford, England, ancestry, until I remembered that my forefathers left England because of religious persecution.

But there was no persecution here as Dr. Latham ushered me into a small room reserved for visiting historians. It had plenty of window light, a large table with chairs, and several electrical fixtures for connecting up my examination equipment.

Then I noticed something that had escaped my eye at first. In the center of the table rested a thick, yellowed document, obviously of ancient vintage, which appeared to measure about 9 by 12 inches in size. Adjacent to this document were two other larger sized documents that appeared to be written on old parchment paper.

"There it is, Mr. Doud," said Latham, pointing to the smaller document, "the last will and testament of Henry VIII." And then continuing with a twinkle in his eye, "Be careful with your examination. England may be forced to take back America if you find Henry's will to be a forgery. Neither one of us would want that, would we?"

After describing the two large parchment documents as "letters patent," thought to bear examples of Henry's drum stamp signature, Dr. Latham walked out of the room, leaving me on my own to answer questions about a priceless document 420 years old.

Impatient to take my first look at Henry's will, I sat down at the table and cautiously turned back the hard cover of the 14-page document. At the top of the very first page was the signature "Henry R" (Rex). I then turned to the last page, and there I found a second signature, this time followed by the names of eleven eyewitnesses to the signing. Why so many witnesses? I thought to myself. Wasn't this overdoing it a bit?

Using my microscope light, now unpacked from my suitcase of equipment, I carefully directed a beam of light through the back side of page one. There in the center of the page was a beautiful watermark design of what appeared to be the royal coat of arms of Henry VIII. Examining the paper more carefully with a 3X magnifier, I could see telltale lines running in only one direction across the surface, indicative of a hand-made "laid" type of production. All other pages of the will were the same.

The fact that hand-made, watermarked papers were used for Henry's will is of more than passing interest since the papermaking process did not become popular in England until a much later time. Hand-made papers were probably a novelty during Henry's reign, with only two of the scores of documents I eventually examined being written on this type of paper.

As interesting as all of this was, two other aspects of the evidence assumed more importance to my examination of Henry's will. The first was to look for indented grooves located in or around the visible ink strokes of the signatures—grooves caused by a dry stamp device being pressed with great force into the surface of the paper. The second was to compare the will's signatures with known examples of Henry's "sign manual."

Tackling first the search for grooves in the signature areas of the will, I expected trouble in trying to separate the ink strokes from the indentations, but I wasn't expecting some of the other complications that arose during my examination.

Indentations in paper are usually imperceptible to the eye under ordinary, indirect room lighting; but when a strong beam of light is thrown parallel to the paper's surface, the grooves running at right angles to the light become clear and legible, similar to the ruts in a country road at sundown.

When I applied this "grazing light" technique to the signatures on the first and last pages of the will, I could find no evidence whatsoever of indented grooves, either within or outside of the ink lines. I also employed other techniques designed to accentuate indentations but with similar results.

Then I noticed something on all fourteen pages of the will that rendered the significance of the missing indentations quite debatable. Under high power magnification, I could see on the back side of each page evidence of a meshlike material applied sometime in the past as a method of preserving the document. When I told Latham of my discovery, he replied, "Oh, yes, we use that kind of material on many of our historical documents." He then suggested that I accompany him on a visit to the laboratory where conservation specialists are employed to preserve and repair ancient documents. What I learned was not only astonishing but revealing of the way British conservators view the restoration and preservation of historical documents.

The first step in the process, I noticed from my perch on a stool next to the chief technician, was to dampen both sides of the document with water. This, he explained, enabled them to smooth out wrinkles and join torn parts neatly together. Noticing my look of disbelief at the thought of applying water before even testing the inks for permanency, Dr. Latham said with a chuckle, "We don't have to worry about that sort of thing in our old documents. They were all written with carbon-based inks that are as permanent as any writing fluid ever invented.

Then, using a large painter's brush, the technician placed a chemically inert wheat paste material on the back of the document, over which was carefully pressed a sheet of semi-stiff silk-mesh material. After a brief drying period, the document with its protective covering was placed in a giant press and subjected to 400 pounds of pressure per square inch.

Insofar as King Henry's will was concerned, no one in the Public Record Office seemed to know exactly when the document was restored to its present condition. But whenever it was, it seemed quite clear that any indentations caused by a dry stamp would surely have been affected by the swelling action of the water on the paper, not to speak of the application of great pressure during the final stages of the restoration.

I also examined two other documents similarly written on handmade paper, similarly preserved with silk-mesh material, and similarly listed in the register as being executed by dry stamp. I could find no evidence whatsoever of the indented markings that must have been present at the time the dry stamp signatures were executed. I also looked for indentations in the parchment documents known to contain stamped signatures but also failed to find anything significant.

On the basis of my examinations and the technology available to me at the time, it was apparent that any argument about missing indentations could now be put to rest. There was no physical evidence as to their existence or non-existence.

But, fortunately, that was only one facet of the problem, and the principal task still remained of comparing the will signatures with the known dry stamp signatures and with known examples of the king's handwritten signatures, most of which, unfortunately, were on documents dated much earlier.

It is axiomatic in the field of questioned document examination that no two signatures of any individual are ever identical. Based on this premise, the document expert frequently testifies that two or more signatures are forgeries, traced from a single genuine signature, his findings being based on a too-close similarity in letter forms, size, slant, proportions, and relationship of component parts of the signature to each other.

The execution of dry stamp signatures involves much the same type of evidence, the only difference being that the pen follows an indented outline produced by a die rather than the illuminated outline of an actual signature placed beneath the questioned document and made visible by transmitted light from a window or light box. Neither type of tracing can possibly result in an *exact* replica of the exemplar signature, the process involving action by the human hand which itself is subject to variation, not to speak of the inability of the hand to follow an outline perfectly. Indeed, the very nature of the indented grooves requiring the use of side lighting to make them visible would inevitably create difficulty for the person attempting to follow the outline and result in periodic departures from the indented guideline.

Initially, the will signatures were compared with each other and with the two known examples of Henry's dry stamp signature referred to earlier. Because of the thickness of the will pages and the fact that they were permanently bound between hard covers, it was impossible to conduct a superimposition, transmitted light comparison of the two will signatures, the most desirable type of procedure for problems of this kind. Accordingly, exact size transparency films or "templates" of the will signatures, which had been prepared ahead of time, were used. By positioning these transparent reproductions over the two will signatures and over the exemplar signatures it was possible to make a detailed exact-size transparent reproduction over the two will signatures and over comparisons of all components of the signatures.

The results of this initial comparison were most illuminating. Except for a few minor deviations in the strokes, the will signatures matched up closely with each other and with the known dry stamp signatures. Indeed, the sandwiched signatures were so much alike that they took on the appearance of one single signature.

A similar comparison of the will signatures and exemplars known to have been signed by the king's own hand disclosed substantial variations in all aspects of the writing, including size and relationship of parts of the signatures to each other.

To verify the results of this examination, I asked a custodian for additional specimen signatures of King Henry VIII. To my great surprise, she located over 100 additional exemplar documents dated during the last two months of Henry's life. Most of these were "letters patent" (commissions or grants of authority) in which, interestingly, the signatures were affixed at the beginning of the documents rather than at the closing. The custodian indicated that most of these documents were listed in

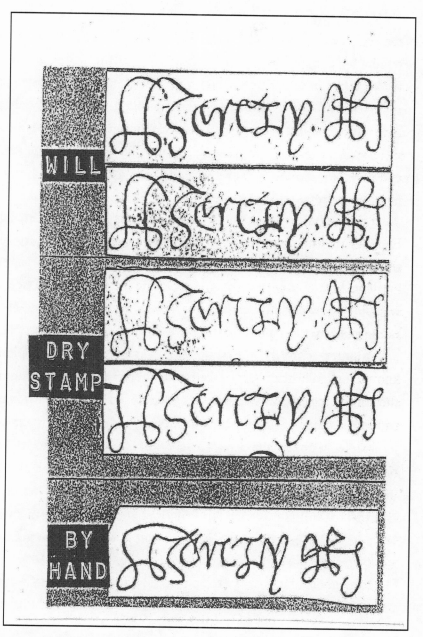

The will signatures (top) and dry stamp signatures (center) are virtually identical. Henry's handwritten signatures (bottom) varied from each other.

the register as bearing dry stamp signatures of Henry VIII.

As before, the transparency templates of the will signatures were placed over the exemplars, and it was no great surprise to find that virtually everyone of them matched up perfectly. The only apparent exceptions were four signatures produced by a different kind of facsimile stamp having the general characteristics of a rubber stamp impression, but which was probably prepared by an embossed wood die operated in conjunction with an inking pad. The appearance of the ink coupled with the exactness of the signatures constituted strong evidence of the nature of the process.

The use of this second type of stamped signature posed a number of rather interesting questions. Was this stamp also authorized by the king; and if so, was its use as highly restricted and guarded as the dry stamp signature? Was the pardon of Clerk and the other custodians charged with "impressing the writing of the king's sign manual" also intended to cover this particular device? If the answer to these questions is no, one is constrained to wonder whether the use of a second stamp on certain letters patent was, in fact, an unauthorized action by one of Henry's unprincipled councilors designed to undermine the monarchy. But this, of course, is mere speculation; and, for the moment at least, there appeared to be no reasonable explanation for the existence of a second stamp.

Insofar as the will was concerned, the existence of some ninety-five signatures dated within the last two months of

A Ghostly Royal Hand
The Mysterious Last Will and Testament of Henry VIII

Henry's life, all of which were virtually identical to the will signatures, did provide a definite answer. While one might conceivably explain the close coincidence of two signatures as an "accidental" occurrence, the cumulative weight of ninety-seven specimens, including the will signatures, having the same general size, spacing, slant, proportions, and letter forms could only have one explanation—that they were all executed by the dry stamp process.

It would appear that loyal supporters of the imprisoned Mary Queen of Scots and others of the Stuart line contested King Henry's will in court sometime after his death. The grounds, presumably, were lack of testamentary capacity, omission of the Stuarts from the royal line of succession, and questions about the legality of the two signatures on the will. The Stuarts undoubtedly suspected the use of a dry stamp.

At the trial, it would appear that counsel for the Stuarts introduced the testimony of a handwriting expert. For what reason one can only conjecture, but it was likely on the subject of the dry stamp. If so, British statutes would surely have limited the scope of his testimony to a mere expression of opinion. The law also made no provisions for the introduction of comparison signatures other than those in the case for some other purpose. With these problems and others shrouded in the silence surrounding Henry's last six hours of life, it is no wonder that the Stuarts lost their case.

Still curious about the will contest brought by the Stuarts and the details of the trial, I wrote to Dr. G. O. Sayles, recommended to me as being the leading British authority on cases involving "The Court of Kings Bench." Dr. Sayles' reply was a masterpiece of understatement, as he wrote in a small, neatly organized script: "It is true that I have…produced six volumes of work regarding records of the Court of Kings Bench from the reign of John, but I stopped at the close of Henry V's reign in 1422. It has taken me over forty years to get that far, but then there is a record of every action that came before the Court, and this sometimes means as many as 6,000 cases in a single law term—a really stupendous task…"

While I was disappointed at Dr. Sayles' inability to supply information on the Stuart will contest, I could only marvel at the persistence of this friendly and single-minded man who was willing to devote forty years of his life to one research project.

Following my return to Wisconsin, I called Dr. Smith at Northwestern University to report my conclusions. He was not surprised at my inability to find indentations from the dry stamp device—he had looked for them himself on an earlier occasion. But he was astonished at the weight of other evidence supporting my conclusion that the signatures were not handwritten by Henry. Ninety-four known dry stamp signatures represented a lot of evidence, and the fact that they all perfectly matched the signatures on Henry VIII's will was most revealing.

There was no question about it—Henry's will was signed by a dry stamp facsimile device and not "by my most gracious hand." But there was still one more tantalizing question to be answered. Were the dry stamp signatures applied to the document *after* Henry's death? The eleven eye witnesses never revealed what happened on that fateful night, nor did any of the others gathered around while the old monarch slipped from life to death. That question may provide fuel for another professorial debate, but I regret to say my expertise is limited to events of the here-and-now and not the hereafter. Had I possessed that ability, I would have been better prepared to tackle the 1971 Chicago voting fraud debacle where many of the signatures were signed from the grave.

9

A Petition Signing Party
in Chicago:
Knaves of the Round Table

The Chicago Democratic machine is well known for its political chicanery around election time, both in local and national contests. Indeed, Democratic ward politicians in Cook County openly brag about the Kennedy-Nixon election where they manufactured enough votes from the cemetery, fake voter registration cards, and stuffed ballots to swing the Illinois election total to Kennedy. Therefore, few eyebrows were raised when, during the 1971-72 elections for State's Attorney, it was announced that *in six hours* workers for Judge Raymond Berg, the last-minute selection of Mayor Daley, had come up with 800 nominating petitions containing 20,000 signatures. Curiously, this was 14,000 more than required by law to place his name on the ballot, a figure cited by Berg as supporting the genuineness of the petitions. Why would anyone forge more signatures than absolutely necessary?

Berg's opponent, veteran States Attorney Richard Hanrahan, saw it otherwise and screamed, "Fraud!" But he, too, had his cross to bear. Under indictment for conspiracy to obstruct justice in the Black Panther case, Hanrahan now suffered the second indignity of being dumped by his old pal, Mayor Daley, as being a political liability. The scene was ripe for another good old Chicago-style free-for-all!

It was around 6:30 PM on a Saturday night in December of 1971. At our home in suburban Milwaukee, my wife and I were getting dressed for a neighborhood dinner party when the phone rang. "This is George Bliss, investigative reporter for the *Chicago Daily News*. Remember me? I have a case I would like you to work on."

Indeed, I did remember Bliss. Ordinarily, I do not accept cases from newspaper reporters, who are frequently more interested in sensation than in facts, but Bliss was a cut above the others. In the Orville Hodge state treasury scandal, we had worked closely together, with Bliss digging up a number of records that proved to be helpful to my forgery investigations and to the Attorney General's case against Hodge.

But now, Bliss explained to me, the *Daily News* had joined forces with a political watchdog organization, the Independent Voters of Illinois (IVI) to investigate the possibility of fraud in the nominating petitions of Judge Raymond Berg. It was hard for them to believe that 20,000 petition signatures could be obtained in a period of only six hours. Would I be willing to examine the signatures on short notice to see if there was any basis for their suspicions? Sure, why not, I thought to myself as I accepted the assignment, little realizing that "short notice" in newspaper jargon meant *right now*.

"This may seem a little unrealistic," continued Bliss, "but we would like to send a messenger to Milwaukee *tonight* with copies of the 800 Raymond Berg petitions and would like you to have an answer for us *by tomorrow morning*. That is the deadline for filing objections to the petition. If our messenger leaves Chicago by 8:00 PM we can have the documents in your hands by 10:00 PM."

"You have to be joking, George," I sputtered into the telephone. "At the most, I might be able to examine one or two thousand signatures before morning, but twenty thousand? That is simply not possible."

"Well, do the best you can," said my caller, who had faced a lot of deadlines himself. "If your examination turns up anything promising, legal counsel for IVI can file our objections tomorrow. At a later time we can give you more time and perhaps obtain genuine signatures from the Board of Election Commissioners for comparison with the petition signatures."

The neighborhood dinner party my wife and I attended that night was a success except for one guest who was totally absorbed in his own thoughts—during all four courses—answering most questions in monosyllables or, to the embarrassment of his wife, not at all. At 9:30 when he left, I am sure the host and hostess breathed a sigh of relief.

On the block-long walk back to our house, I mentally reviewed some of the other petition cases I had examined in the past and tried to develop some kind of a plan for examining at least a representative number of the 20,000 Berg petition signatures. As I turned into the driveway to our house, my thoughts were interrupted by the sight of a young man standing at the front door clutching in his two arms a stack of documents fully a foot and one-half tall. Obviously anxious to be relieved of his burden, he quickly followed me through the front door and into the dining room where he plopped his burden down on the dining room table with a resounding thud. "There you are, Mr. Doud," he said, as he quickly retreated through the door. "Have a good night."

I have examined many problems involving the authenticity of petition signatures during my fifty-year career as a forensic document examiner, and most of them are difficult, stress-producing cases to resolve. Genuine signatures are not available for comparison purposes, at least in the early stages of the investigation; and, with the exception of family names, the signatures on the petitions to be compared usually contain different upper and lower case letters. The street addresses, also required by law, offer the best hope of reaching some conclusion, especially if the alleged signers live on the same street. The circulator's signature at the bottom of the page must also be compared with the names and addresses of petition signers. Again, the examination usually involves the almost impossible task of comparing unlike writings.

Undaunted by the huge stack of documents before me, I pulled my chair up to the dining room table and plunged into the unknown. Using a 3-power magnifier, I started with the first petition at the top of the stack, examining and comparing signatures and addresses one with the others. Nothing appeared suspicious, although the different names and streets made the examination quite difficult. Examination and comparison of the circulator's name and address didn't add anything to the examination. The second petition from the top was much the same. "Inconclusive," I put in my notes regarding this page.

On the third petition from the top, I found two names, obviously man and wife, signed by the same individual. I have found this to be a common phenomenon in virtually all of the election petitions I have examined. Even though each person circulating a petition is required to sign the statement, "I do hereby certify…that the signatures on this sheet were signed in my presence and are genuine," signature "forgeries" by family members inevitably occur.

At this point in the examination, I decided to save time and energy by concentrating on entries having similar street names that could be more readily compared. To my surprise, these were few and far between, and when I did find them, the comparisons produced nothing of real significance.

It was now 12:00 AM and I could hear my wife returning from the neighborhood party and bubbling over with news and gossip. "That'll have to wait 'til another time, dear," I said, anticipating what was sure to follow. "I have been working on this darn problem for two hours now and have only covered twenty-five of the petitions. At this rate it will take me 'til 6:00 AM to examine one-eighth of the petition signatures, and I'd better get hopping."

Like any other monotonous job, examination of hundreds of signatures can be exceedingly tiring and stressful, Always in the back of one's mind is the thought: "Stay alert or you might miss some important piece of evidence." So now, two hours later at 2 in the morning, I was getting very tired—and very discouraged. Were Bliss and the IVI wrong in their suspicions about the petitions? Was I asking too much of myself to help to uncover anything in an examination having such extreme time constraints?

I leaned back in my chair and closed my eyes, hoping to find in the solitude some answer to this puzzle. Then out of the blue came a possible answer that made so much sense that I wondered why in the world I hadn't thought of it before. Why, of course, with only six hours to obtain the 20,000 signatures, any forged entries, if they did indeed exist, would be more likely to occur at the end of that period, when the urgency to complete the petitions was highest, rather than the beginning. Since the petitions were numbered consecutively according to the time in which they were received at the Board of Election Commissioners, the ones at the bottom of the stack rather than those at the top were likely to be the most significant. So I did what I should have done much earlier—I turned the entire stack of documents upside down and started examining signatures from the bottom.

As I recall it today, the first petition I examined contained signatures with addresses on "Grenshaw St." Although I couldn't quite put my finger on it, there seemed to be something strange about the entries. Some of the addresses looked too much alike to have been written by different individuals. Then it hit me like a bombshell. The reason they looked alike was that every sixth address was written by the same person. I was flabbergasted and elated all at the same time. I had heard about "round-tabled" petitions, and apparently this was another example of that peculiarly Chicago election device.

Suddenly I was no longer tired, and for the next hour I examined page after page of fraudulent petition signatures and

Portion of one "round tabled" petition. Six individuals were involved in filling out all the entries, one of whom wrote the addresses indicated by arrows.

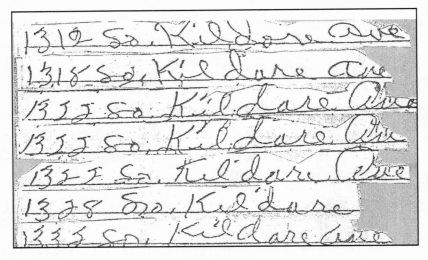

Addresses from two other petitions, all written by the same person.

addresses, all of them round-tabled. In some cases, six people were involved in the plot; in others, five. In my mind's eye, I tried to recreate the scenario for the events that took place. Perhaps held in a smoke-filled room at Democratic headquarters in Chicago's 24th Ward, groups of precinct workers were invited to a traditional round-table exercise, much like the one envisioned by King Arthur but with a slightly different motive. At each table sat five or six people, each with a list of names, perhaps obtained from polling lists or in some cases from the telephone or other directory. Worker number one started it off by placing a name and address on line one, followed by workers number two, three, four, and five, and so forth until the page was filled. As the petitions were completed, they were immediately rushed down to the Board of Election Commissioners to meet the deadline. By 4:00 AM I had discovered over 400 round-tabled signatures and finally decided to call it quits. As I was preparing for bed, I told my wife, who was now wide awake, "Dear, somebody in Chicago had a Raymond Berg petition signing party. At each table were six people, and in some cases five, who must have had writer's cramp by the end of the evening. Don't make any plans for the next few days, I suspect I will be very busy."

The following day, within hours of my report to George Bliss and the Independent Voters of Illinois organization, headlines in the *Chicago Daily News* screamed in inch-high type, "FORGERIES ON HALF OF BERG PETITIONS," accompanied by a photograph of me, perhaps obtained from newspaper morgue files. I was not pleased with either the headlines, which misrepresented the scope of my examination, or the photograph. But I must admit, basking in the limelight for a few days had certain redeeming features.

As frequently happens in Chicago politics, the round-tabling scandal erupted into a series of investigations into every aspect of the voting process, including the procedures employed by the Board of Election Commissioners to ensure the legitimacy of all elections. To no one's surprise, the Board failed to find over 8,000 signed voter's applications for registration, which could have been used to compare with the 20,000 petition signatures.

While all of this was going on, interviews were being conducted of some of the alleged signers and circulators of the petitions. Among the strange things investigators for IVI found was the name of Eugene Graham who had died months before the petition drive and that of Jim Hurd as circulator of the same petition, who was out of town at the time and could not possibly have signed anything.

Ultimately, the Cook County State's Attorney's office entered the picture and employed me to examine over 300 "Certificates of Registered Voters" for Ward 24, supposedly signed by individual voters in the presence of election judges. In the subsequent trial before Federal District Court Judge Bernard Decker, I testified that most of the certificate signatures were forged by the election judges themselves. Three of the group were sentenced to two-year terms; the other two were slapped on the wrist with sentences of "five nonconsecutive weekends in the county jail's work release program." In the end, fourteen election judges were convicted and sentenced to various prison terms, which may be a record for Democratic politics in Cook County. As for Raymond Berg and his round-tabled petitions, the Illinois Appellate Court ruled that, although massive fraud existed in many of his petitions, IVI had failed to prove forgery in at least 6,000 of the signatures. Raymond Berg, who appeared to be an innocent victim of all the chicanery, lost to Richard Hanrahan by an overwhelming margin in the primary election for State's Attorney.

10

A Gallery of Clowns

A Gambler, a Long-Lost Daughter, and a Strange Will

Similar to the mysteries unraveled by Sherlock Holmes, my work as a forensic document examiner depends upon the interpretation of evidence, the elimination of clues that may be incapable of rational explanation, and the acceptance of one final solution. The case involving the last will and testament of gambler Laurence Wakefield involved that kind of evidence.

$500,000 FOUND IN HOME," screamed the headline in my *Chicago Tribune* for February 20, 1964. The accompanying article went on to describe how a Chicago fire department rescue unit and a policeman assigned to them had responded to an emergency telephone call from a woman identifying herself as Mrs. Rose Kennedy Wakefield. "Come to my house immediately; my husband is having a heart attack," she was quoted as saying.

The south side Chicago address given to the operator proved to be a modest, single-family brick home similar to many others on the block. But there the similarity ended, for the contents of the home were far from ordinary. While the rescue unit struggled to revive the desperately ill Laurence Wakefield, the young policeman who had finished his paperwork noticed a large number of coins scattered throughout the living room. When he lifted some newspapers on a table, he told *Tribune* reporters, "I found underneath rolls of coins, maybe $50 or $60 in nickels, dimes and quarters." Suspicious that the money might have some gambling connection, he called for more policemen from nearby Kensington precinct station. When they arrived, things really got interesting. One of the officers, while poking around various parts of the house, forced open the door to a back bedroom. To his utter astonishment, there lay before him one of the largest caches of money ever to be recovered by Chicago police. Scattered about the floor, in dresser drawers, boxes, and even in laundry bags was over $750,000 in $1, $5, $10, and $20 bills (the initial *Tribune* estimate was $250,000 short). "I almost fainted," one officer was quoted as exclaiming. "The money was everywhere, all over the room—everywhere but on the ceiling."

When questioned about this enormous hoard of money, Wakefield's wife professed ignorance about its origin, but a search of police files and other available records disclosed more revealing information: Laurence Wakefield, it would seem, had been a "policy wheel operator" in the early days when blacks ran most of the gambling operations in Chicago. When the Al Capone era gangsters took over syndicated gambling in Chicago, Wakefield wisely decided to reduce the size of his operation and save his money for the uncertain future that lay ahead. And save it he did. His frugal lifestyle convinced neighbors, former gambling friends, and, indeed, the US Internal Revenue Service that he was poverty-stricken. But little good came from Laurence Wakefield's penny-pinching ways—he died an unhappy, reclusive man shortly after arriving at the hospital, with only Rose and a few gambling buddies to grieve over his demise.

The *Tribune* story ended on a significant note. While the search of the gambler's house had turned up lots of money, no will could be found anywhere. Laurence Wakefield, it would appear, had died intestate, leaving his fortune to the vagaries of the law and Chicago politics.

Like many other readers of the initial *Tribune* story, I became intrigued with the disposition of the $750,000 gambler's hoard. Did Mrs. Wakefield stand to inherit all of her husband's estate despite the absence of a will? Were there other direct descendants of Laurence Wakefield from previous marriages? What about claims against the estate by his old-time gambling connections or their Capone-era successors? The answer was not long in coming.

Three days after Wakefield's death, a second *Tribune* headline announced, "COUNT $763,000 POLICY HOARD" (another upward revision this time of $13,000). The accompanying article revealed some interesting details. After deducting an IRS penalty of $102,000 for Wakefield's failure to pay federal gambling taxes and a $3,000 Cook County delinquent gaming tax, $628,000 remained for Wakefield's sole heir, his wife, Rose Kennedy Wakefield. Unfortunately for Rose, this optimistic prediction proved to be a little premature.

To my surprise, and presumably the surprise (and elation) of other readers of the *Tribune*, a third follow-up article described the fate of Rose Kennedy Wakefield's claim. It would appear that the gambler's companion of twenty-five years was not married to him after all, even though they had lived together as man and wife. Rose's claim against Laurence's estate was definitely in jeopardy. Indeed, at a Circuit Court hearing to decide the disposition of Wakefield's estate, Judge John S. Boyle took care of Rose Kennedy "Wakefield's" claim in one succinct ruling: "Mrs. Kennedy has no legal claim to the estate as Wakefield's common-law wife. Common-law marriages are not recognized in Illinois."

A few days after this surprising development, a familiar voice was on the telephone calling me from Chicago. "Mr. Doud, this is Attorney Norman C. Barry—do you remember me?" You bet I remembered him! A handsome, outgoing man in his early forties, son of one of the most respected judges in Chicago, Barry had consulted me on previous occasions. When he mentioned the name "Wakefield" during the course of our conversation, I knew I was in for another blockbuster.

As counsel for the Cook County Public Administrator's office, Barry had been investigating the claims of fifteen people representing themselves to be relatives of Laurence Wakefield. Apparently alerted by the *Tribune* articles to the possibility of "sharing" in Wakefield's bounty, most of the claimants tried but failed to produce convincing evidence of any family connection. But there were exceptions. One of the most prominent was a young woman, "Constance Beverly Wakefield," who claimed to be a daughter from Wakefield's early marriage to Edith Jarvis Wakefield, now deceased. Another was Rose Kennedy (Wakefield) who, undaunted by Judge Boyle's earlier ruling, still persisted in her attempts to acquire Wakefield's estate. The last was a joint claim by nine cousins of Wakefield's mother, which seemed to have some basis in fact. Nevertheless, judging by sheer numbers of supporting documents submitted to the court, the claim of Constance Beverly Wakefield appeared to be the strongest and, at the same time, the most mysterious of all.

In support of her claim, Constance Beverly Wakefield produced two wills, dated in 1943 and 1962, both of which left most of Wakefield's estate to her. Other documents supporting her relationship to Wakefield were also submitted, including a "Remembrance of First Communion" signed by the pastor of Wakefield's church.

"This sounds like a pretty straightforward case," I mused to myself as Barry reassured me that I would have plenty of genuine signatures of Wakefield to compare with those on the wills. All of the documentary evidence was to be delivered to my Chicago office early the following day.

"Is this some kind of a joke?" I thought to myself the next morning as I took my first look at the 1962 will and tried to struggle through the illiterate, crudely written provisions of the document. "And where are the Laurence Wakefield signatures Norman Barry had asked me to examine? It took a bit of searching before I finally found two tiny names apparently intended to authenticate the unusual document. The first, signed "Laurence Wakefield," appeared on the top line following "In the name of God, Amen. I, ..." and the second, with the addition of the initial "W" appeared about three-quarters of the way down on the left side following the words, "Signed, sealed, published and declared to be the Last Will and Testament of..." words intended to describe the requirements for witnessing the will. The dotted testator's line where Wakefield's signature should have appeared was occupied instead by the name of the notary—an alleged eyewitness to Wakefield's signing. The only logical thing about this illogical document was the correct placement of the names and addresses of the three witnesses in the lower part of the document.

"This 1962 will must go down as one of the strangest documents ever to be examined by a forensic document expert," I thought to myself as I finished my preliminary study of the document. But there were more surprises to come.

Crudely hand printed on an old school examination form, the

1943 will contained about the same provisions as the 1962 document, but my eye was immediately drawn to the name "Laurence Wakefield" and the address, "2941 Ellis Ave." appearing in the lower left corner of the document. Both were written in the same kind of petite handwriting evident on the 1962 will. But size alone would not necessarily condemn the signatures. Some individuals habitually write quite small, but was this also true of Laurence Wakefield? His genuine signatures would be the final arbiter of that question.

The genuine writings presented for comparison purposes are the lifeblood of any signature examination. They should be plentiful enough to reflect the individual's habits of writing under different conditions and close enough in date to minimize the chance that some change may have occurred in the writing due to age or ill health.

Examination of Laurence Wakefield's genuine signatures revealed the writing of a moderately skilled individual who had developed a number of individualities in his signatures. The writing was of normal size. Where there was a limited space of signing, such as the two-inch space on the back of a check, Wakefield would use two lines rather than attempting to squeeze his signature into a single line.

Using a low-power magnifier, I commenced a detailed examination of the signatures on the 1943 and 1962 wills. "Unnatural, clumsily drawn, containing all of the classic evidences of forgery," was the way I described these awful looking signatures in my notes. When compared with genuine signatures of Wakefield, the results were even worse. Not only did the two sets of signatures differ in writing habits, but the will signatures were only about half the size of Wakefield's genuine signature, even though the space for signing was comparable. Obviously, something was badly amiss! The drawn, unnatural appearance of the signatures was understandable—that was due to attempted imitation—but why the diminutive size?

Using my 10-power stereoscopic microscope, I then discovered evidence that added another dimension to the investigation. Running alongside the principal ink lines of the will signatures, I could see clumps of pencil graphite clinging to the paper fibers. The pencil outline appeared to have a simple explanation: the signatures were forged by the tracing method. In this type of forgery, a genuine signature and the document to be traced are sandwiched together over a window or light. The illuminated image of the genuine signature is then traced onto the questioned document and used as a guide for production of the final ink signature. The pencil remnants may or may not be erased from around the signature.

Infrared ray photography is a common method of revealing and demonstrating the presence of pencil underneath an ink signature. Indeed, in some cases—such as the Laurence Wakefield signatures where washable inks were used—the infrared ray may miraculously eliminate the ink strokes entirely, leaving only the pencil tracing outline.

One of the features of my work that I find most exciting is the piecing together of different facets of evidence, rather like a jigsaw puzzle, in order to reach a rational, scientific conclusion. Sometimes the final piece of the puzzle merely adds weight to already existing evidence; but like most other scientists, I am reluctant to drop an investigation before I know *all* the answers. The will signatures were tracings, of that I was sure, but tracings from what? Harry Cassidy of Richmond, Virginia, a good friend and humorist in the vein of Will Rogers, once told me, "Don, most document examiners spend too much time fussing around trying to force solutions to problems. If they would just put their feet up on the desk as I do and close their eyes, their questions would be answered in due time, including some they were not even asking." Well, I can't vouch for the last part of Harry's remarks, but when I closed my eyes and mentally put myself in the place of the forger of Laurence Wakefield's signature, the answer suddenly dawned upon me: Why, the model for the tracing would have to be a reduced size microfilm or photocopy signature, one readily available to a potential forger. And where would a signature of that kind be found? Most likely in the Motor Vehicle Department, the Register of Deeds office, or in the Bureau of Vital Statistics.

When I informed Attorney Barry of my suspicions, he said, "Okay, I'll start right away sending around for reproductions that might meet your description." And so it was, after the second or third try, that I received in the mail the document that was to provide the final piece of the puzzle—the death certificate of Edith Wakefield, Laurence Wakefield's mother. Her son Laurence had signed his name as informant near the bottom of the document. There could be no question about it. When I made a transparency film of this tiny, microfilm-produced signature and placed it over the signatures on the 1943 and 1962 wills, they superimposed almost exactly—except for the initial *W* that appeared on two of the four will signatures and not on the death certificate.

But even this difference had a reasonable explanation. Deciding for some reason that two of the signatures on the wills required a middle initial, the forger simply shifted the paper slightly during the tracing process to accommodate the extra *W*, which was traced from the *W* of "Wakefield". The "Laurence" and "Wakefield" portions of the names superimposed closely as did the "2941 Ellis Ave." address on the 1943 will.

The first communion document purporting to show that Constance Beverly Wakefield received first communion in Wakefield's church proved to be half good and half bad. The bad part was a radical erasure of the original name on the face of the document, which was replaced with the name "Constance Wakefield." The good part was the genuine signature of the church rector, J. C. Stuart, who officiated at her first communion. But even this was not all good, for his signature was itself traced over (perhaps to obscure the evidence) and in turn used as a model for tracing the J. C. Simard signature as witness onto the

Death certificate of Edith Wakefield, Lawrence Wakefield's mother. Note Lawrence Wakefield signature near bottom of left side.

227

1943 will. As for the alleged witnesses to the signing of the 1962 will, they either could not be found or professed ignorance about signing their names to any will of Laurence W. Wakefield.

In the end, all claims of Constance Beverly Wakefield were summarily dismissed by the court on the basis of my report and other impeaching evidence. Because of allegations of mental incompetence, Constance was not tried on a forgery charge. Ultimately, a court settlement awarded $431,385 to Mrs. Rose Kennedy, the Chicago-style rationale being "for her contributions to Wakefield's gambling enterprises," and $60,000 to the county as contraband. The balance of $270,000 was set aside for payments of future expenses and claims, among them a federal income tax lien for $102,000. Thus ended this bizarre saga of illegal money, a common-law wife, and a most inept forger.

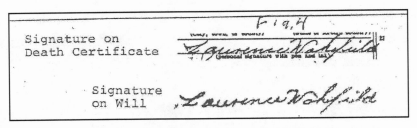

Comparison of Lawrence Wakefield signature on death certificate, and signature on questioned will.

Less Than Holy Ghost:
Handwriting from the Grave

I have had many unusual courtroom experiences in my fifty years as an expert witness, but none more strange than one involving the death benefit claim of Bruce Hower, a Gary, Indiana, undertaker, against Fireman's Fund Insurance Company.

I should, perhaps, have been forewarned that something unusual would happen in this outrageous case, for when I entered the courtroom awaiting my turn to testify, my eyes were irresistibly drawn to the plaintiff, Bruce Hower, a distinguished looking black man dressed in clerical garb. In addition to a reversed white collar, he sported a large silver cross at least six inches in height that swung from his neck and reflected mirror images that danced about the courtroom as he moved. Nobody had bothered to question Hower about the source of his ordination, or indeed if he had been ordained at all. What did emerge from trial testimony was that, for a price, Hower would not only embalm and bury the body but would also provide a complete religious service in any denomination desired. It was too bad that the poor wretch in the casket couldn't appreciate this "all service" treatment, which in fact was designed as a means of making Hower rich at the expense of insurance companies. The many nameless derelicts who happened to drift

229

into Gary and die there were simply unwitting allies.

It would be immodest to say that my testimony that afternoon completely demolished the claim of Bruce Hower that one Frank Henderson, an itinerant black worker who ended up in the Hower Funeral Home as the result of a railroad accident, had previously signed an accident policy naming him (Hower) the beneficiary. My testimony was to the effect that Hower and not the dead man had signed the Frank Henderson names on the policy application and other insurance documents.

I can still recall the unwavering, hypnotic stare of the plaintiff during the course of my testimony, which grew particularly intense at the end of cross-examination when his young attorney asked me what proved to be one too many questions. Holding up for my view a picture of the dead man lying in his coffin, the cross-examiner asked, "Mr. Doud, if we don't have any genuine signatures of Frank Henderson to compare with the names on all these insurance documents, how can you be so sure that he didn't sign them?"

"Oh, I have one very good reason," I replied.

"You mean to tell me that from this photograph you can say that Mr. Henderson could not possibly have signed the application for insurance and the other renewal documents? Please tell this jury again, Mr. Doud, how you reached this astonishing conclusion."

"I reached that conclusion because it was *Bruce Hower* who forged the Frank Henderson names and, therefore, it is obviously impossible that this man lying in the casket could have done so."

While this ill-advised question ended my cross-examination, it was not to be the end of my exposure to the unpredictable Bruce Hower. At the conclusion of my testimony, the court recessed for an afternoon break, and I stepped down from the witness stand, intending to talk briefly with my counsel and thereafter leave the courtroom. I had not taken over five steps when I glanced up and saw the clerically garbed plaintiff walking toward me with a determined and unsmiling look on his face and a hand in his right pocket that bulged ominously. I involuntarily leaned back against the jury box. Is he about to shoot me? I thought to myself. Should I request help from the bailiff? But now, as he approached until only a few inches separated us, a faint smile crossed his face as he removed his clenched right hand from his pocket, opened it up, and laid it gently upon my shoulder. "God bless you, brother," he said. "I hold no malice towards you."

I can still remember my mindless response, which really made no sense at all unless viewed as a reaction to the sense of relief I had suddenly experienced. "Are you an ordained minister?" I blurted out. Bruce Hower, undertaker, minister, friend to the friendless, all rolled into one, just smiled and walked away.

Caught in a Time Warp

It was straight out of a true-science magazine: the witness, Dr. Irving Goodman, deftly fielding questions from the cross-examiner about the many devices he had invented throughout the years—emphasizing how he sent himself self-addressed, registered letters to memorialize the dates of first conception of each invention. He then described in detail how in September of 1948 he had developed the dual nozzle compressed-air device that sprayed polyester resin from one nozzle and chopped-up fiberglass strands from the other. The unique part of this device, proclaimed Goodman with a wave of his hand, was the use of ordinary, single-sided razor blades, installed in a rotating head, to cut the fiberglass. He had made further improvements to the design in November of 1949.

Turning his head to smile ingratiatingly at the judge, Goodman testified that his device would "revolutionize" the manufacture of fiberglass boats, caskets, and personalized objects such as prosthetic devices. Then, reaching over to the two self-addressed envelopes resting on the judge's bench, Goodman turned them over and pointed to the two postmarks stamped at the junctures formed by the top, side, and bottom flaps of each envelope. "You can see the postmark dates, September 8, 1948, and November 8, 1949," he told his questioner. "That's when I sent the letters to myself." Then, anticipating the next question, Goodman volunteered, "They have always been sealed while in my possession until a few days ago when I was ordered by the court to slit them open to see what was inside.

Goodman smiled as the cross-examiner retreated to the counsel table, seemingly about to terminate the questioning. But then the atmosphere in the courtroom turned from friendly to hostile. "Dr. Goodman," barked the attorney as he approached the witness box and jerked the registered letters from the witness's hands, "Isn't it true that these envelopes which I hold in my hand originally contained details of entirely different inventions? Sometime after 1955 you steamed open the side flap of each one, took out the original material and substituted the documents relating to your so-called polyester-fiberglass invention—*isn't that true?*"

I was sitting in the front row of the spectator's area with patent attorney Patrick Hume of Chicago for whom I had examined the self-addressed envelopes and enclosures earlier that morning, an examination that revealed some most interesting and startling evidence! The REGISTERED stamp on the left side of the 1948 envelope was badly distorted in four areas: the second *E* of 'REGISTERED," the *8* of "1948" and the alignment of both inside and outside circles. The stamp at the right side of the envelope was normal in all respects. On the 1949 envelope, certain areas of the left stamp were similarly distorted, and the ones on the right undisturbed. This evidence plus traces of glue extending over the margins of the side flaps provided overwhelming evidence that the left sides had been opened, probably by steaming, and then imperfectly resealed with new glue. A staple had also been punched through the left stamp of the 1948, obviously designed to obscure evidence of the distorted printing.

One of my routine tasks as a questioned document examiner was to keep abreast of any changes in ink formulations that might be significant in dating documents. In the case of the handwritten notations inserted in Goodman's envelopes, I used a very simple test. I bleached the color from microscopic areas of the ink strokes and then viewed the results under ultraviolet light. The ink glowed spectacularly. It was of a unique, fluorescent type first manufactured by the Parker Pen Company in 1955. Dr. Goodman would have a lot of explaining to do about this seven-year discrepancy in dates.

The question just asked the witness about steaming open and resealing the side flaps of the envelope "sometime after 1955" was one I had helped prepare for the attorneys. But I, and seemingly everyone else in the courtroom, was totally unprepared for Goodman's startling response.

Trembling from head to foot with beads of perspiration breaking out on his forehead, the witness staggered to his feet, clutched the left lapel of his coat with one hand, the other raised in supplication to some deity unknown, and slowly crumbled to the floor of the witness box. From our vantage point in the spectator area, all Hume and I could see were twitching feet protruding from one end of the witness box. The judge, from his elevated position, could obviously see the whole show, as could the court reporter. Yet, the courtroom was eerily silent—no one rushed up to assist the inert man.

It probably was only seconds, but it seemed like minutes, before the judge finally remarked in a calm voice, "Well, perhaps someone should go upstairs and have the paramedics bring down a stretcher to carry Dr. Goodman to an ambulance." Turning to his clerk, he said, "Would you mind doing that, John?" At this precise moment, the double doors at the back of the courtroom were flung open by a dowdy little lady dressed in a bright print dress who screamed as she ran down the aisle, "Irving, Irving, something has happened to my Irving," and rushed to the witness stand to comfort her fallen warrior. I was not the only one to wonder how she knew that "something had happened to Irving." No one had left the courtroom during this period of time, including the judge's clerk who had not yet started on his mission to first aid. Obviously, Goodman and his wife had not rehearsed their act very well. The heroine in a Gilbert and Sullivan comic opera would have timed her appearance much better than that.

But the best was yet to come. Two young paramedics finally arrived with their stretcher and tugged and pulled the moaning figure from behind the witness box and onto the stretcher while Mrs. Goodman clucked and fussed alongside. As the paramedics passed my position on the front bench, I could hear her say to the one in the lead, "Who's going to pay for this, anyway?"

As far as Irving Goodman and his "invention," he and his bumbling accomplice left Miami for New York, following a hospital stay of extraordinarily short duration. He was never called back by any of the parties to the patent dispute, who were probably content to leave things well enough alone. The judge apparently decided it was too much bother to charge him with anything.

11

Blindman's Bluff:
Justice Also Was Blind

*It is an old maxim of mine that when you have excluded
the impossible, whatever remains, however improbable,
must be the truth.*

ARTHUR CONAN DOYLE, *Adventures of Sherlock Holmes*

The upper loop of the *h* in "Ruebush" was guillotined as
neatly as the head of Mary Queen of Scots. But unlike that
unfortunate woman's cranium, I was able to scientifically
reattach the missing member and thereby establish one link in a
chain of evidence that led to overwhelming proof of forgery.

Sherlock Holmes would have loved this kind of
investigation, having its beginning with one tiny clue, which his
arch rivals from the Metropolitan Police would surely have
missed, and then discovering another, and another, and others
that literally branded a cleverly manipulated document as being
a forgery. Holmes's bitter enemy Moriarty would, of course, be
mixed up in the crime but deny everything. The readers of this

chapter are urged to decide whether the physical evidence of forgery is strong enough to finally bring Moriarty to justice.

Fred Ruebush was a farmer living with his wife near the little northwestern Illinois town of Sciota. While his health was fairly good for a man in his late eighties and he was able to move about and take care of most of his affairs, Ruebush's eyesight became progressively worse. In 1962 when he finally visited an optometrist, the diagnosis was "no recordable vision."

Fred Ruebush died in early 1963 at the age of eighty-nine, following which the administrator of his estate took steps to probate his will and expeditiously distribute the proceeds.

But Ernest Simpson, a farm hand who had worked for Ruebush on and off for several years, had other ideas. He marched into probate court with a $60,000 claim against the Ruebush estate based upon a promissory note dated February 21, 1959, payable to himself and signed by Fred Ruebush. Anyone wishing to challenge the validity of the note, said Simpson, might wish to consider that two other farm workers, Oscar Rauch and Paul Hampton, were also present at the time and signed their names as witnesses.

Shocked by this unexpected turn of events, the administrator for the Ruebush estate began an investigation into the background of the claim with its supporting document, the $60,000 promissory note. I was contacted early on by the attorney for the Ruebush estate to make a preliminary examination of photocopy documents, with the understanding that I would later have access to the original note and additional known specimens.

When the photocopy of the $60,000 promissory note finally arrived by mail at my Chicago office, I found it to be surprisingly good—good enough, at least, to reveal an important clue about the document's execution. The signature "Fred Ruebush" and address "Sciota Ill." were skewed in a diagonal direction across the lines of the form, typical manifestations of writings by the visually handicapped.

And exactly what was the condition of Ruebush's eyesight in February of 1959? The optometrist who examined Ruebush's eyes in 1962 was again contacted and reported back that his own records showed no previous visits by Fred Ruebush, nor did the records of other eye specialists contacted in the Sciota area.

But all was not lost, said the optometrist. What he could not do from records of prior eye examination he could do almost as well by *diagnostically* turning back the clock to February 21, 1959. At that time, he reported, Fred Ruebush would have had "very limited" vision—certainly not good enough to drive a car or to read fine print such as that appearing on a promissory note. He could make that statement with some confidence, because the degenerative eye disease with which Fred Ruebush was afflicted commonly deteriorated the eyesight in a predictable manner. Glasses, apparently worn by Ruebush from time to time, could have aided his failing eyesight, but only marginally.

The legal battle began with subpoenas for depositions being served on claimant Ernest Simpson and on the two alleged witnesses to the signing, Oscar Rauch and Paul Hampton. As to

the origin and execution of the $60,000 note, their deposition
testimony ran substantially as follows:

> The weather on February 21, 1959, was below
> freezing, and it had snowed lightly the night before.
> It was about 1:30 PM and they could all see
> Ruebush's old 1947 Ford parked next to a
> warehouse building located on one of his farms
> known as Camp Ellis. Rauch and Simpson said they
> saw Ruebush drive his Ford into the Camp Ellis
> property, presumably from his home in Sciota.

Hampton told a different story. It was Ernest Simpson who
drove Ruebush to the farm. He saw them in the car together.
According to Simpson and Rauch, the promissory note form
itself was provided by Fred Ruebush, who personally selected
the unusual site for its execution—the hood of his old Ford.
Because of dirt and moisture on the hood, Ruebush placed an
envelope of some kind under the document so that the writings
on the face would not be affected. All of the men wore gloves.
What next took place is best described in Simpson's own words
from his deposition:

> Fred Ruebush asked Oscar [Rauch] if he'd fill it
> out. He said he didn't have his glasses with him,
> and couldn't see well enough to do so. [Note: Rauch
> also confirmed that Ruebush was not wearing
> glasses at the time]. Oscar told him he didn't know

too much about it and he told him he'd tell him what to put on it and so Oscar laid it on the front of his Ford and filled it out.

Simpson's testimony that Rauch filled in the body of the note confirmed, in part, the results of my earlier examination of photocopy evidence—with one exception. The payee's name "Ernest Simpson" on line three, I had reported, was *not* filled in by Rauch but by Simpson himself. I had found a perfect match between Simpson's known signatures and the name inserted on the note. And what would Simpson have to say about this potentially explosive issue? "Sure, I inserted my own name on line three," he said, "I guess I thought that Oscar Rauch wouldn't know how to spell it—anyway, what's the big deal, as long as Fred Ruebush saw me doing it." His memory jogged, Rauch also recalled leaving line three blank at Simpson's request.

"What bizarre testimony," I thought to myself. "The lawyers should have a lot of fun with this on closing argument."

The pre-trial depositions of Simpson, Rauch, and Hampton finally got around to the central question: How did the signature "Fred Ruebush" and the address "Sciota Ill." get on that promissory note? Oscar Rauch testified that, after filling in the body of the note, he personally saw Fred Ruebush take out his ball pen and write his name and address on the note. Immediately thereafter, Rauch stated, he signed his own name as witness. Paul Hampton had a somewhat different story to tell.

He was in the nearby warehouse building at the time and did not actually see Rauch fill in the document or Fred Ruebush sign it. All of the writing was on the note at the time he signed as witness. Simpson's testimony was the most ambiguous of all. While it was true that he inserted his own name on line three as payee, he couldn't remember seeing Fred Ruebush actually sign the note. He did seem to remember, however, that Ruebush picked up the document from its resting place on the hood and held it about six inches from his eyes, apparently to read what was on it. One thing Simpson knew for sure—Ruebush handed him the promissory note directly after it was completed, and he kept it in a strongbox at the bank ever since.

The consideration for the note, according to Simpson, was certain debts run up by Ruebush through purchases of livestock and machinery, plus a promise he made to run Ruebush's Camp Ellis farm for him until the time of his death. Central to the whole deal, Simpson claimed, was the understanding that after Ruebush's death he would arrange with the heirs for an exchange of the promissory note for the Camp Ellis property.

Ruebush's widow and children were astonished at the testimony of Simpson, not to speak of Rauch and Hampton. They knew of no financial transactions between the deceased man and Simpson other than payments of his monthly salary and some minor sales of machinery and livestock that Ruebush promptly paid for. In addition, they, and everyone else in Sciota, knew how tight-fisted and shrewd old Ruebush was. He would be the last one to let a hired hand operate any of his farms, not to speak of virtually giving one away under the terms described by Simpson.

With the two sides miles apart in their versions of the case and the battle lines drawn, the status of the $60,000 promissory note began to assume more and more importance. Was it a genuine document or was it forged? I had gone as far as I could with the photocopies, and I now needed to examine the original note in order to unlock any further evidence it might contain.

Appearing at my Chicago office one warm day in August of 1963, the attorneys for both Simpson and the Ruebush estate delivered the hotly contested promissory note to my care with the same formality one might expect from a loan of the Star of India diamond. I guess I have always been impatient with unnecessary legal protocol, and the jockeying around by the attorneys, presumably to assure the safety of this document, made me extremely uneasy. I wanted to get on with my examination, not to listen to a lot of legal wrangling over the meaning of a court order. Finally rid of my tormentors, I carefully slit open the sealed packet now resting on my desk and took my first look at a document that was to consume much of my attention for the next two weeks.

I had examined writings of the visually handicapped before and found each case to be unique and challenging. In one case involving the suspected forgery of a signature, I had blindfolded myself in an effort to recreate the circumstances of writing while blind. The signatures I produced turned out to be poorly aligned relative to the lines on the rule pad but reflecting my usual writing habits. The evidence relating to Ruebush's name and address on the promissory note for $60,000 involved a much more complicated scenario.

Examining the document first with a three-power hand magnifier and then with a stereoscopic zoom microscope, my first impression was of genuineness. The poor alignment of the Fred Ruebush signature and Sciota, Ill., address confirmed my earlier observations about Ruebush's failed eyesight. Now I had even more concrete evidence at my disposal—a number of known signatures and other writings of Fred Ruebush executed in February of 1959. I found every one of them to be poorly aligned and running through the lines of the forms. Despite these distortions, they still contained the identifying habits of Fred

Promissory note signed by Fred Ruebush. Misalignment of the Fred Ruebush signature and the Sciota, Ill. address are consistent with other known signatures of Fred Ruebush, which were also poorly aligned. Note the missing top to the "h" of "Ruebush"

Ruebush who, I was forced to report to my disappointed client, also wrote the Fred Ruebush signature and address on the $60,000 promissory note.

Then I placed my microscope over the missing top to the "h" of "Ruebush." Was this gap in the letter due to a ball pen ink failure or to some other cause? I had written a technical paper on the skipping characteristics of early ball pens, noting that this phenomena usually occurred when the rolling ball suddenly reversed directions or struck an oily surface such as a fingerprint. But this was different. Most of the loop to the "h" had been sliced off as though by a knife, but with the ink in the surviving left stub slightly lower than the right. To add to the intrigue, when I turned my high intensity light source from vertical to horizontal in order to view the *h* by grazing sidelight, as one would view a rutted country road at sundown, I could see an *indented* outline of the missing top to the *h*. When I zoomed my microscope to its highest setting, I could also see within the indentation four faint, crater-like formations. Two were at the ends of the cut-off stubs and two were near the top of the loop, at the left and right sides.

Then my eye was drawn to a faint horizontal line running precisely through the juncture of the visible and indented portions of the *h* and out to the right edge of the paper. What was that all about? Again using the grazing sidelight technique, I could see evidence of paper fiber disturbances in the area immediately above that line.

I next examined the area below the printed material on the left side and immediately ran across three other areas of fiber disturbance. The first one contacted the *w* of "witness," the second, less prominent, example was located above the *u* of "Rauch," and the third ran through the top of the *f* of "Hampton." In each case I found telling evidence of paper fibers being wrenched upright by removal of Scotch tape. The other alternative would have been abrasive erasures, and I could see no evidence of paper thinning or residues of rubber eraser left imbedded in the paper. The fiber disturbances I had found were due to removal of Scotch tape and nothing else.

The contacting points between the fiber disturbances and the writings of Rauch and Hampton were important from another standpoint. When I viewed the areas under high magnification, the evidence was overwhelming that the handwriting was placed on the document *after* the removal of the Scotch tape. The ink strokes stained and clearly overlapped the disturbed paper fibers. By way of contrast, Ruebush signed his name while Scotch tape was still attached to the document.

The excitement began to build as I realized the possible implications of what I had just discovered. Could it be that some other piece of paper was taped over the text of the promissory note in order to hide it from Fred Ruebush's view at the time he signed and then removed for the signatures of the two witnesses? I could hardly wait to explore that theory.

When I placed an 8½ by 2½ inch straight-edged piece of

paper over the printed text of the document, with lower edge extending just over the last line of printing beginning "which said Bank" and ending, "deposit accounts," the results were most revealing. Lo and behold, the three areas of paper fiber disturbance were positioned directly below the paper edge, and, like the Royal Guard during the queen's inspection, they all lined up perfectly in a row. Was this mere coincidence or, perhaps, evidence that Scotch tape had been used in these three locations and in the signature area to attach some other document to the upper part of the note?

With my theory now gaining a lot of plausibility, the ultimate test would be the effect of that same paper edge upon the beheaded *h* of "Ruebush." Just as I suspected, when I followed that edge to the right side of the document, it crossed directly beneath the top two craters in the indented loop. It also contacted the peak of the *b* of "Ruebush," but because of a blob of ink at that point I was unable to tell whether or not a crater had been formed. But I still had another ace in the hole—infrared photography, which sometimes produces miraculous results in photographically removing unwanted material from a document. I used a deep red filter over my camera lens, a film sensitive to the infrared, and a grazing sidelight directed from various angles. I could hardly wait to see what the developed negative would show. To my delight, when I held the film up to a light source, the ink had completely disappeared. All that remained were indented grooves of the *b* with a crater at the very top where the pen had struck something that impeded its progress.

The implications of those mysterious craters finally struck home. Why hadn't I thought of it before? The lower craters at the ends of the cut-off stubs of the *h* were caused by the ball pen contacting the edge of the Scotch tape on its upward and downward journey. The faint horizontal line running across the stubs plus the disturbed paper fibers immediately above the line were artifacts left behind after the removal of the Scotch tape.

The top two craters must have been created by the ball pen as it contacted the edge of the paper Scotch-taped to the note—the paper meant to hide the note's provisions from Fred Ruebush's eyes. A similar event must have occurred at the top of the *b* where Fred Ruebush's ball pen contacted the edge of the offending paper.

The clues were piling up. But were they enough to prove beyond a shadow of a doubt that old Fred Ruebush signed his name to a fraudulently conceived document? I needed to conduct my own tests to see whether I could duplicate the evidence I had just observed.

So-called parallel testing of evidence such as that I conducted in the Ruebush case requires a replication of all elements bearing on the execution of a questioned document. It may also involve testing procedures to verify or discount statements made by alleged eyewitnesses.

The experimental materials I used included examples of Table Grove promissory note forms supplied by the bank itself, samples of other note forms of comparable thickness and composition, ball pens capable of producing the same type of strokes I had observed in Fred Ruebush's name and address, envelopes of various kinds, and Scotch tape samples.

I also contacted the Minnesota Mining and Manufacturing Company (3M) to learn all I could about the composition and characteristics of Scotch tape products—how various types of tape affected the paper surface when they were applied and when they were removed. How did age and soiling affect the performance of Scotch tape products? The technical personnel of that company couldn't have been more helpful in providing answers to virtually all of my questions. I now had everything before me to conduct experiments that I fervently hoped would resolve any lingering doubts.

In order to verify or discard my theory that the upper part of the note was covered over at the time Fred Ruebush wrote his name and address, I again used an 8½ by 2½ inch piece of straight-edged paper, placing its bottom edge over the last line of printing on my test note form. I then taped the paper to the note, applying the tape in exactly the same areas where I had detected fiber disturbance on the original.

In the area of Ruebush's signature, I attached the test paper to the note with Scotch tape running lengthwise and with the bottom edge of the tape positioned precisely where that faint line appeared on the original. If my theory was correct, this was the condition of the note as it was presented to Ruebush for his signature. It was now time to place myself in the shoes of Fred Ruebush as he wrote the letter *h* in his signature over the Scotch tape-paper combination.

With ball pen poised for action, I was almost tempted to squint my eyes in order to approximate the condition of Fred Ruebush's eyes at the time of signing. Instead, I needed all of the eyesight I could muster to try to replicate the exact relationship of the loop of the *h* to the Scotch tape attachment, and this required a lot of practice.

It was while I was making a series of experimental loops that I first discovered another important aspect to the problem—the tactile responses I felt in my fingers as I executed the writing. For example, on its upward journey to form the right side of the loop, my ball pen first struck the edge of the Scotch tape, where my fingers felt a slight resistance and momentary stoppage of the pen before proceeding to the next level. There it struck a second impediment, the edge of the test paper taped to the note. As before, my fingers could feel a slight resistance to the pen's progress as it momentarily stopped and jumped another level.

On its downward journey to form the left side of the loop, my fingers felt a different reaction to the ledge-like formations. As my pen jumped *down* from the edge of the test paper and from that of the Scotch tape, I could feel slight jolts, as one's body might feel, in greatly magnified form, while walking down steps. Would the gloved hand of Fred Ruebush have felt the same thing my fingers did? Perhaps, but unless he was concentrating on the writing act, as I was, his suspicions would not likely have been aroused.

Now came the acid test for my experiments. Having duplicated the theoretical conditions under which Fred Ruebush wrote the *h* in his signature, I now must remove the Scotch tape to see what evidence had been left behind. When I stripped it off and microscopically examined the area by grazing sidelight, I could scarcely believe my eyes. The crater-like formations I had discovered earlier in the questioned *h* were replicated almost exactly.

Insofar as the faint horizontal line was concerned, the soiled edge of an old roll of Scotch tape I found in my bottom drawer supplied the answer, as did its removal from my test paper, which produced fiber disturbances similar to those I had observed on the questioned document. The three areas of torn paper fibers on the left side were readily reproducible by applying the Scotch tape with varying degrees of pressure and removing it with vigor or with care.

I now had persuasive evidence as to how Fred Ruebush's signature and address got on that $60,000 promissory note: someone had taped another piece of paper, perhaps a wage receipt or some other innocuous document, *over* the printed information on the note. With his bad eyesight, Fred Ruebush signed the document, not realizing he was affixing his name to a different kind of document obligating him to pay Ernest Simpson the sum of $60,000 "at death."

In the cases I examined throughout the years, I often applied the so-called "theory of probability" to the clues I discovered during the course of my examinations. Could they possibly be accidental in nature or due to some innocent coincidence, leading me in turn to an erroneous conclusion?

When I applied that theory to the Fred Ruebush case, involving as it did over a dozen clues all having a rational explanation and pointing to the same conclusion, I could state with scientific assurance that the note in question was a contrived document meant to cheat a semi-blind old man out of $60,000. Like building a brick wall where each brick adds a vital support to the final product, my conclusions not only met the test of probability but of positive proof as well. The readers of this chapter may judge for themselves whether there are any chinks in my wall.

The trial of Ernest Simpson vs. the Estate of Fred Ruebush took place in McComb, Illinois, before Circuit Court Judge Edwin Becker. I testified for the better part of a day about the evidence I had discovered, using numerous photographic exhibits similar to those illustrated in this chapter. Judge Becker followed my testimony carefully and seemed particularly interested in my demonstrative evidence, which I had felt all along was overwhelming and unassailable.

Cross-examination was directed, as I had anticipated, on the possibility that the evidence of Scotch tape removal was due to abrasive erasure and that the missing top to the *h* was somehow or other due to the flap of the envelope allegedly placed under the document while it was being signed. What nonsense! Even if the flap had been uppermost, it could not possibly have resulted in the beheaded *h*, the faint horizontal line, the torn paper fibers, and evidence within the indented grooves. Judge Becker made it quite clear that he was unimpressed with this pie-in-the-sky type of cross-examination, and Simpson's lawyer soon quit in frustration.

At the conclusion of the trial, Judge Becker disallowed the entire claim of Ernest Simpson as being based upon a fraudulently conceived document and lacking in proof of consideration. He also added a few choice words about the ethics of those who would take advantage of an old, semi-blind man.

With such overwhelming proof of fraud and such a forceful opinion from Judge Becker, the executors of the Ruebush estate were prepared to put the Simpson case behind them and complete probate of the Ruebush estate.

But Ernest Simpson and his lawyer saw things differently and decided to appeal the verdict to the Illinois Appellate Court. There they had found out something that I had known for a long time. The Illinois Appellate Court didn't like forensic handwriting experts and had come down with a slew of opinions supporting that conclusion. They stood a good chance of having Judge Becker's opinion reversed, irrespective of the evidence.

Ordinarily, in taking up an appeal from a lower court decision, appellate courts do not concern themselves with reading hundreds of pages of testimony from the original trial.

Their duty largely is to rule on admissibility of evidence, application of the law to certain situations, and citing other upper court opinions relating to the evidence in the case.

In his opinion reversing Judge Becker's findings and remanding the case for a new trial, Appellate Judge Scheineman, writing for the three-court panel, viewed himself in a larger role. Taking upon himself the burdensome task of reviewing trial transcripts and apparently trial exhibits as well, the justice ended up confusing conjecture with facts and misconstruing some of the testimony. For example, in connection with the name "Ernest Simpson," which Rauch, Hampton, and Simpson himself had *admitted* was written by Simpson, the justice stated, "In the presence of Simpson and one Rauch, *Ruebush* got the note out of the car, placed it on the hood, *and wrote the name Ernest Simpson as payee.*'

But the most illogical attack on appellant's evidence was reserved for my testimony, about which the justice had this to say:

> It was the handwriting expert's opinion that the smudges on the note were caused by scotch tape which may have attached something over part of the note above the signature, and that it had been removed before the two witnesses signed. He based his opinion largely on apparent jumps, or blanks, in the lines of the signature, and stated he had experimented with strips of scotch tape on paper.

He made no mention of experiments under stated conditions, such as an envelope under the paper, to see if a pen crossing the flap of the envelope would cause a similar jump or blank.

The latter statement showed a complete failure on the part of the justice to understand the reason for the indented top to the *h*.

Further on in his opinion, Justice Scheineman quoted from that most outrageous of all appellate court decisions, Jones vs. Jones:

> Expert testimony has its useful place, but being an opinion, it has less weight than direct testimony on a controverted fact... To do so would put a premium on secondary evidence, not justified by any rule of law.

Ultimately, the Ruebush case was tried a second time by a different Circuit Court judge. My testimony as well as that of the other witnesses was much the same as in the first trial, with only two or three exceptions. In my case, Justice Scheineman had made such a big fuss about the envelope allegedly placed under the note at the time of signing that I felt it necessary to conduct extensive experiments using both the flap and smooth sides of the envelope. The results were negative. Neither the front nor back of the envelope affected the writing on my sample promissory note, including the indented top to the *h*.

But all of this was to no avail. As is frequently the case in a retrial of a case reversed by the Appellate Court, the Circuit Court judge ruled in favor of Simpson and the $60,000 promissory note. A second appeal to the Illinois Appellate Court resulted in the same decision as rendered by the first, without the extensive commentary indulged in by Justice Scheineman.

Thus ended a fascinating case, but one in which I fervently believe a terrible miscarriage of justice was done. To add insult to injury, I was personally involved in the will contest of Jones vs. Jones, on which both of the Appellate Court rulings in the Ruebush case relied. A decade earlier, while mentoring under Herbert J. Walter of Chicago, I had made up the signature comparison exhibit for Walter's use in court. That same comparison exhibit became central to the Illinois Appellate Court's vituperative decision.

Was the court's decision upholding the validity of the signature on the will correct? Or did it create a bad legal precedent based upon an even worse forgery? In a later chapter dealing with H. J. Walter and my experiences working in his office, readers will be able to study the exhibit I prepared and make up their own minds.

12

Paying Homage to My Mentors: They Made It All Possible

H. J. Walter of Chicago was one of three remarkable individuals with whom I trained in the forties. They were all early pioneers in the field of questioned document examination and advanced the profession in countless ways.

From Leopold-Loeb to Hauptmann-Lindbergh to Al Capone, my three mentors testified in most of the notable document cases of early years. They educated those courts who would listen, and the general public to a new kind of expert testimony based upon demonstrable reasons for their conclusions. They laid the legal groundwork for all of us who followed in their footsteps.

The telling of their stories and mine requires a journey back in time to the first half of the twentieth century and my entry into the profession at the very end of that period.

Super-Star of the Hauptmann-Lindbergh Case: Clark Sellers was a Pioneer in the Use of Demonstrative Evidence

Outfitted in my new, on-sale, double-breasted grey suit from Bullocks Department Store, polka-dot blue tie, new shoes that squeaked when I walked, and a pallor common only to prison inmates and sanitarium patients, I must have been quite a sight to the illustrious Clark Sellers. A handsome, impeccably dressed man in his late forties, slightly on the stout side, with thinning brown hair and a ready smile, it was easy to see why Sellers had become somewhat of an icon in the questioned document field. Any secret reservations he might have felt about hiring this unconventional job applicant were kept well hidden. With a backlog of trial preparation a mile long, he obviously needed me more desperately than I needed him.

Not surprisingly, much of my time during the first year of my five-year stint with Sellers was devoted to making comparison exhibits for his use in court. This was a tedious, time-consuming job of cutting letters or words from photographs of questioned and known material, identifying the documents from which they were taken, and pasting the cutouts side by side on an appropriate background material. Finally, mural-size photographs of the charts were prepared for Sellers's use in court.

These were tasks in which Sellers and I consulted every step of the way, for he had very definite ideas about the way the exhibits were to be designed and presented in court. On rare occasions, he would completely tear apart something I had been working on, saying, "Don, this isn't right—it's going to be too confusing for the jury to understand." As frustrated as I was at the time, I almost always had to admit that the alternative he suggested would be much better. In the area of demonstrative evidence and effective expert testimony, Sellers was a pioneer and unquestionably the best in the business.

The 1935 trial of Bruno Hauptmann for the kidnaping and murder of the Lindbergh baby illustrates Sellers's genius for capturing a jury's attention through innovative testimony and easy to understand comparison exhibits. As the last of eight handwriting witnesses called to testify for the State of New Jersey, Sellers had a huge problem to overcome: Having listened to day after day of testimony about the fifteen ransom notes, the jury was simply bored to death with the handwriting issue.

Realizing his dilemma, Sellers attacked the problem head-on by first gaining their attention through a startling admission: Hauptmann's known writing *differed* from the handwriting on the ransom notes in a number of respects. He paid a lot of attention to those differences, said Sellers, because he didn't want to make the mistake of accusing Hauptmann of writing the ransom notes when he didn't do it. In the end, however, he was literally forced to the conclusion that the differences were due to attempted disguise and not to the writing habits of some other person. This display of concern for the fairness of his examination then led Sellers to a discussion of the similarities he had found in the writings and the evaluation process he went through in finally deciding that Hauptmann was guilty of writing the ransom notes.

Now wide awake, the jury was ready for those wonderful, easy to understand comparison exhibits which Sellers explained in the simplest of terms. Concluding his testimony with a chart comparing a genuine signature of Hauptmann's with letters from the ransom notes, Sellers stated, "Hauptmann might just as well have signed his name to each one of the ransom notes, so convincing is the evidence that he did write them." The newspapers reported the next day that *anyone* could see that Hauptmann wrote the ransom notes. In the end, Hauptmann was found guilty of kidnaping and was put to death in the electric chair.

I was fascinated by the handwriting evidence in the Hauptmann-Lindbergh case and spent many hours studying Sellers's office files and the comparison exhibits mounted on his office walls. From them I learned some very fundamental facts about handwriting that I have never forgotten. First and foremost is the persistent nature of adult writing habits that renders it virtually impossible for anyone to maintain a successful disguise throughout an extended amount of writing. In Hauptmann's case, his early German schooling, before learning English in America, made it doubly difficult for him to disguise his ransom note

Dear sir!
Have 50,000$ redy 2500$ in
20$ bills 15000$ in 10$ bills and 10000$ in
5$ bills. After 2-4 days
we will inform you were to deliver
the mony.
We warn you for making
anyding public or for notify the polise
the child is in gute care.
Indication for all letters are
        singature
                and 3 holes.

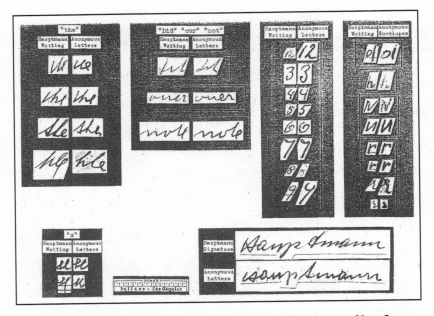

A comparison exhibit used by Sellers at the 1935 Flemington, New Jersey, trial of Bruno Hauptmann. The caption "Anonymous Letters" was used to denote the ransom notes.

handwriting. It was full of strange letter forms such as the *x* made like a double *ee*, the *g* with angular, open top, and the printed *d* appearing like a *0 1* combination. Other characters like the *t* crossed at the bottom and the two-stroke *a* were pure accents from his German writing background. These and other identifying similarities led me irresistibly to the conclusion that Hauptmann and no one else wrote the fifteen ransom notes.

I also learned something else from the Hauptmann-Lindbergh case. It was Sellers's demonstrative evidence as much as his testimony that convinced the jury that Hauptmann wrote the ransom notes. His comparison charts were absolutely vital to the jury's understanding of the evidence, enabling them to see with their own eyes the connecting link between Hauptmann's writing and that on the ransom notes. Sellers's powerful exhibits had taken handwriting testimony out of the realm of mere opinion evidence and into that of demonstrable proof.

This was Sellers's legacy to me and to the profession. Not once during my later career as a handwriting witness did I ever appear in court without some kind of demonstrative evidence.

A Smile Brightens My First Day in Court

As time went by, I gradually broadened my horizons in the Sellers office—examining cases, drafting reports, doing more research, and assisting him with trial details. But now, after five years in his employ, I was planning to resign to make room for David Black, Sellers's former associate, finally back from his Navy tour of duty. For a year, Sellers had been promising me the opportunity to testify for the first time, but the "appropriate" case never came along—until now—just as I was about to leave.

The case involved calendar entries relating to a real estate transaction—entries that were supposedly written chronologically, on separate days during the month. Not so, said Sellers in his report. All thirty entries looked too much alike to have been written in that fashion. Now it was my job to reexamine the evidence in order to reach my own conclusion. As I opened the case file Sellers had placed on my desk, I secretly wondered what he would say if I reached a different conclusion from his, heaven forbid. But the evidence was clear-cut, even to my inexperienced eye. It was just not possible for entries supposedly written on thirty separate occasions to look so much alike in the inks used, the placement of the entries in the boxes, and in the sameness of the writing. Daily entries for other months differed markedly from the ones in question.

When I arrived in court and stumbled up to the witness stand, comparison exhibits in hand, my mind suddenly went blank—I had forgotten everything I was going to say, and I was prostrate with fear. In a letter sent a few days later to my mentor-to-be Herbert J. Walter of Chicago, I described a miraculous recovery: "I testified in my first case on Tuesday and, although I wouldn't say I covered myself with glory, I think I did an acceptable job. I nearly had heart failure when I discovered that the case was being tried before a jury and not a judge, but upon closer inspection I noted that the members were mostly young ladies, which to a bachelor like me was like an oasis in the desert. When one of them smiled at me during my testimony, I became positively eloquent, and thereafter forgot to be nervous."

The young attorney who cross-examined me appeared to be as inexperienced as I was, and his questions showed it. He just didn't know how to cross-examine an expert witness about a subject he had never even heard of in law school. He didn't even ask me the question I dreaded most, "How many cases have you testified in, Mr. Doud?"

At the close of the short trial, the jury quickly came out with a verdict supporting my finding that the calendar entries were contrived by the plaintiff (to support his version of the case.) I was elated. Not only had my finding been vindicated, but the missing link in my qualifications had been taken care of. But little good would come from my newly gained confidence unless I found a new employer.

I first started corresponding with Herbert J. Walter during the latter part of my stay with Sellers. Always interested in the young people entering the profession, Walter would send me study materials of various kinds and encourage me when I became depressed or bored with my limited duties in the Sellers office. Now that I was about to leave Sellers's employ, Walter wrote that he had "some ideas" to discuss with me about my future as a questioned document examiner. We could, perhaps, talk about them during the forthcoming conference of the American Society of Questioned Document Examiners (ASQDE) to be held in Los Angeles. I knew all about the ASQDE. Sellers had just taken office as president for the 1947-1950 term, and I had helped him set up time slots for the various speakers. At the same time I discovered some amazing things about the background of this illustrious organization.

Founded in 1941 by Albert S. Osborn, dean of the profession, the ASQDE was the first of its kind in the United States.

Composed of about fifteen members from all parts of the United States, Canada, and one from Cuba, all were in private practice. The watch-words during Osborn's term as president were work, study, and testing for proficiency, usually in the areas of handwriting or handprinting. All were designed to improve each member's capabilities as a questioned document examiner.

The early meetings were held at Osborn's home in Montclair, New Jersey, and as host he established rules of conduct that would be hard to imagine or to enforce today. He forbade the use of tobacco or alcohol at any time during the meetings and established a curfew for the members so that they would be rested and at their best the following day. While Osborn was a hard taskmaster and sometimes treated his fellow members more like pupils than equals, his stern goal of striving for excellence still carries on in the ASQDE today. One of the proudest moments of my life was to be sworn in as its eighth president in 1964.

Meeting H. J. Walter for the first time at the Biltmore Hotel conference site was an experience I will never forget. A transplanted Englishman who had migrated to Canada and ultimately to Chicago, "H. J." stood out from all the other attendees. Thin as a rail, erect as a palace guard, and wearing a shirt with a high, starched collar, Walter had all the appearance of an austere British schoolmaster. But there the similarity ended. Far from being austere, he greeted me warmly on the first day of the conference and at every break in the program sat down with me to discuss everything from my health situation to my visions for the future. I must admit, I completely fell under the spell of this fatherly man. Walter had recently suffered the loss of his own son and partner, and I liked to think I was being "adopted" as a way of assuaging his own grief. Adopted or not, I had no idea of the extent to which Walter had gone to assure my future as a questioned document examiner.

Taking my arm during one break, Walter led me across the room to meet a smiling, rotund, balding man in his forties. "Don," said Walter, "I would like to introduce you to Albert D. Osborn of New York. He has a proposal to offer you." To my astonishment, the "proposal" was an invitation to come back to New York to work in the Osborn office for several months. I would be able to handle my own cases, including testimony in court when that became necessary. No darkroom work would be required because Osborn employed a permanent photographer. The great Albert S. Osborn had died the year before, but his son Albert D. Osborn had developed an enviable reputation of his own, and I could hardly contain my excitement at the thought of working for him. When Osborn and I sat down to discuss the details of our association, I was quite amazed to find that he and Walter had worked everything out—everything but the effect a move from sunny California to cold New York would have on my health. A telephone call to my doctor took care of that: "Do what you have to do, Don, but for heaven's sake get plenty of rest," he said. In the meantime, my new-found friend, H. J.

Walter, had left Osborn and me in the room alone, apparently fearful that he would be hugged in an entirely un-British manner.

Albert D. Osborn—Heir to a Dynasty

It was a cold, blustery day in December of 1947 when I arrived by train at Grand Central terminal in New York. Osborn had arranged for me to stay at the St. George Residential Hotel, which, he stated, "can easily be reached by subway." This was my first experience with New York subways, and it was to leave a lasting impression. It was around 5:00 PM and crowds of people were rushing madly through the turnstiles and onto the station platform where the train had just arrived. Desperately hanging onto my suitcase, I was pushed like a heifer in a slaughterhouse hallway through an open door of the jam-packed train. Then, to my utter disbelief, I felt a foot in the small of my back pushing me through the fast-closing door. "Get your ass in there," snarled the attendant. "Wanna get it chopped off?"

This was but one of many wild experiences I had with New York subways and New Yorkers, many of whom lived by a code of conduct that was, to say the least, foreign to my West Coast upbringing. Later on during my stay in New York, I moved to a small room in historic Brooklyn Heights. Someone said that George Washington once lived in a building down the street. If so, that might explain why, in that famous picture of Washington crossing the Delaware, he looked so comfortable while the enlisted men in the boat appeared to be freezing to death. Washington was conditioned to the cold by living in one of those old, clammy, unheated buildings where I stayed!

But there was one advantage to living in Brooklyn Heights—it was only five minutes by subway to the Woolworth building in lower Manhattan where A. D. Osborn had his office. Indeed, the subway exited inside the building itself, and the elevator was only a few steps away. This was one of the few conveniences I ever found in New York. In other respects, all things seemed designed to make life difficult, especially for the uninitiated. There were crowds and line-ups for everything including restaurants and stores. When I finally got to the head of the line, they were usually out of what I wanted. In the courthouse where I testified several times during my stay with Osborn, lawyers were noisily milling around like herds of bleating sheep. How justice was ever administered under these abominable conditions I do not know. I spent New Year's Eve of 1947 in Times Square among scores of boisterous celebrants, yet I never felt more alone in my life.

Things moved at a slower and more orderly pace in the spacious and well-equipped Osborn office and laboratory located on the 33rd floor of the Woolworth Building. Despite a workload that was easily double that of Clark Sellers, A. D. Osborn always seemed unflappable and on top of his cases. Much of the routine work involved insurance company problems such as disputed signatures on change of beneficiary forms or insurance applications, and both he and I were relieved that I could take over some of this burden. The darkroom work was performed, thank goodness, by Osborn's long-time photographer, Mr. Dean, so I could concentrate my attention on examining cases, helping prepare certain cases for trial, and studying reference material. Most of the latter emanated from the fertile mind of A. S. Osborn and correspondence he had initiated with fellow document examiners from all parts of the world. The files in the Osborn office were a treasure-house of information, and I spent many of my Saturdays and evening hours going through them. A. D. Osborn also encouraged me to conduct my own examinations of his cases, from which I gained additional practical experience and confidence in my own findings.

Masterworks Unmasked:
The Harnett-Peto Art Forgeries

My desk in the Osborn office was in a small alcove off the main lobby. From this vantage point, I could watch all of the people entering and leaving the office. One day in February of 1948, the front door literally burst open and in bounced a short-statured, baldheaded, disheveled little man carrying, under each arm, packages that were almost as big as the man himself. Met by Osborn at the door of his private office, I could hear our visitor say in a voice charged with excitement, "Mr. Osborn, I want you to look at the signatures on these Harnett paintings. If you find what my research tends to indicate, it will represent one of the greatest art forgeries this country has ever seen."

Osborn glanced in my direction and, sensing from my wide-eyed expression that I was as curious as he about this volatile man and his "art forgeries," beckoned me over and said, "Don, why don't you join Mr.—Mr.— ..."

"Frankenstein, Alfred Frankenstein's the name," barked our visitor, "art critic for the *San Francisco Chronicle*."

Osborn continued, "Mr. Frankenstein, this is my associate, Mr. Doud. If you don't mind, I would like to have him take some notes about the background of your case."

And take notes I did for the better part of an hour while our visitor paced up and down, first looking out the window, then marching over to the opposite wall and back again. Gesticulating wildly to emphasize a point, he would pause for a moment to jab a finger in the direction of paintings piled up on Osborn's examination table, then continue on in machine-gun fashion to further expand upon his fascinating story.

Working under a Guggenheim fellowship, Frankenstein had been researching the life and works of William Harnett, nineteenth century still life artist. His paintings were to be found in many of the major museums across the country including the Metropolitan, Smith College Museum, Museum of Modern Art, and many others. On the art market, Harnett's paintings commanded prices at that time (1948) of $30,000 and upward.

One of the mysteries Frankenstein hoped to unravel was the use by Harnett of two different styles of painting—the first a "hard style" with crisp, sharp images, and the second a "soft style" with less contrast and more diffused strokes. Art historians had accepted the fact that, for his own reasons, Harnett painted interchangeably in the two divergent styles. After all, they reasoned, Harnett would not be the first artist to vary his painting techniques from time to time. Others have adopted this practice since time immemorial, if nothing else but to confound the art critics or to titillate the public. But apart from the stylistic difference, most historians concluded that the similar use of memorabilia plus the way objects were arranged on the canvas pointed to Harnett as being the author of both soft and hard style paintings. And, of course, there was that unique Harnett signature appearing on the hard style paintings that seemed to be replicated in the soft style works of art—the unusual monogram with the *W* and *M* placed between the upper and lower segments of the goalpost *H*, followed by the smaller upper case letters of the remainder of the name *HARNETT* which were unique in their own way. Differences? Of course there were differences, said the experts. After all, these signatures were painted onto the canvas with a flexible brush which would naturally be more variable than writings with pen and ink. Wide differences between signatures were to be expected—or were they?

Dates appearing on the paintings posed another problem. With but few exceptions, the hard style paintings featured dates placed below and to the right of the signature. Most of the soft style paintings were undated. This omission apparently was not considered suspicious by Harnett collectors and historians. Neither was an even more unusual discrepancy. Harnett died in 1892 yet the envelopes depicted on two of the soft style paintings bore cancellation stamps dated in 1894 and 1900. This anachronism in dating was attributed by one collector to a little surrealistic joke on Harnett's part.

During the course of his research in the East, the name of an obscure artist and friend of Harnett's, John Frederick Peto, was given to Frankenstein. Peto was also a still life painter and was undoubtedly influenced by Harnett's work when both lived in Philadelphia during the late 1800s. Peto later moved to Island Heights, New Jersey, where he continued to paint until the time of his death in 1907. On a hunch, Frankenstein decided to visit Peto's daughter, Mrs. George Smiley, who still lived in her father's Island Heights studio. In his 1953 publication *After the Hunt*[1] (my autographed copy is inscribed: "For Donald Doud—who helped"), Frankenstein writes: "What I found there almost knocked my socks off." For on shelves and wall-brackets in Peto's workshop were the very candlesticks, pistols, lamps and other objects represented, over and over again, in paintings attributable to William Harnett. Had Peto purchased these objects from Harnett at auction, or were they given to Peto as gifts when

---

1. Alfred Victor Frankenstein, *After the Hunt; William Harnett and other American Still Life Painters 1870-1900* (Berkeley: University of California Press, 1953).

he left Philadelphia for New Jersey? Neither possibility seemed likely since Harnett continued to paint still life objects long after Peto had left Philadelphia. But a discovery even more incredible was now occupying Frankenstein's attention. "Gradually," he wrote in *After the Hunt*, "I began to notice the innumerable paintings by Peto that were perched on the ledges, hung on the walls, and stacked in odd corners of the studio." Peto, it would seem, had not only possessed some of the Harnett models, he had also incorporated them into his own still life paintings. Frankenstein also tells of writing a letter to his wife the night of his discovery in which he says: "This house is full of William Michael Harnett's models. It is also full of paintings by John Frederick Peto. There is a connection between them, but I don't know what it is."

Back in Osborn's office, there was a momentary pause in Frankenstein's hour-long monologue—a pause so unexpected that both Osborn and I were, like hypnotized subjects, suddenly jolted into reality. Had our visitor run out of gas? No, he was just shifting gears—into a quieter, more reflective mood. "Gentlemen, I think I am beginning to understand the stylistic connection between some of these Harnett paintings and the use of objects I found in Peto's studio. Now it is up to you, Mr. Osborn, and you, Mr. Doud, to tell me what you can about the signatures. "By the way," he concluded, pointing to the two packages resting on Osborn's laboratory table, "the five paintings in the stack at the left are known to contain genuine Harnett signatures, and those at the right are the ones in question. I'll let you decide whether they too are genuine." Then, as quickly as he had entered, our visitor dashed out into the waiting room, pausing only long enough to shout in our direction, "For God sakes, gentlemen, take good care of those paintings. Most are on loan, and if something should happen to them we will all be in big trouble!"

Whew! I thought to myself as Frankenstein's footsteps echoed down the hall, now for a few moments to loosen my tie and relax from the effects of that whirlwind of a man. But Osborn, now as charged up as Frankenstein, said, "Don, this is a fascinating case. Let's get going on it right away." Gesturing in the direction of the paintings, he continued, "The first thing I want you to do is take all the paintings labeled "known" and those labeled "questioned" and segregate them according to their appearance, whether soft style or hard style. That shouldn't be too difficult, should it?"

Now, if he has asked me that question today after being married to an artist for over fifty years, I would have approached the task with some confidence. But all I could think of at that time was: "Ye, Gods, I'm supposed to be an expert in handwriting, not in painting styles. What do they mean by hard and soft styles? Is a softer brush used for the soft style painting?"

Surprisingly, when I took the artworks into the laboratory and placed them side by side, the difference between the two styles became quite apparent. Objects were crisp and well defined in the hard style paintings; more blurred and foggy in the soft style. I could also see differences in the kinds of models used, and my thoughts returned to Frankenstein's reaction to the memorabilia he discovered when he visited Peto's former studio. But the real bombshell came when Osborn and I compared the William Harnett *signatures* on the hard style paintings with those on the soft style examples. Every single one of them differed in some respect. For example, the sides of the *H* were straight in the soft style paintings rather than being curved inward, the letters *ARNETT* were aligned near the baseline of the monogram *WMH* rather than towards the top, the lower right leg of the *R* curved upward and not downward, and the crossbars to the two *t*'s were disconnected.

Under the microscope, most of the Harnett soft style signatures appeared labored and unnatural with many of the lines being made up of several strokes. The strokes of Harnett's hard style signatures were made continuously and literally proclaimed genuineness by the uninhibited way in which they were painted on the canvas.

I glanced over at Osborn, knowing that he had reached the same conclusion I had and was trying to fit the final pieces of this jigsaw puzzle together. First, we knew from our examination that the William Harnett signatures on the hard style paintings were genuine and those on the soft style, forgeries. If the technique used for the soft style paintings and the objects portrayed in them were consistent with the work of John Frederick Peto, we were

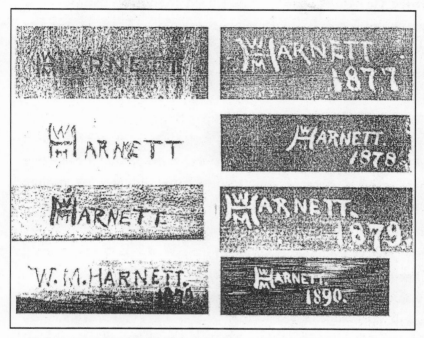

Comparison exhibit I prepared for Albert D. Osborn. Forged signatures are in the left column; genuine Harnett, on the right.

likely to find a painted-out name *Peto* on the canvas. How to uncover it?

With the soft style paintings now evenly divided between us, Osborn and I pondered the possibility of using ultraviolet or infrared techniques to penetrate the layer or two of covering paint one would expect to encounter if our suspicions held true. Infrared had the best chance of working, but it involved a long, drawn-out photographic process, and we needed results as fast as possible. Then Osborn introduced me to a procedure he had used in the past to decipher colored handwriting blocked out by a coating of dark ink. Using a variety of colored filters, sometimes in combination, with illumination directed from various angles, we searched the lower-right area of each painting adjacent to the forged name *WMHarnett*. It was frustrating work, and I was unable to find anything in the first paintings I examined.

Finally, I heard Osborn exclaim, "I think I found one. Come over here, Don, and take a look." As Osborn rotated the painting to get the best angle of illumination, I could suddenly see through one of my colored filters what he saw—a faint shadow outline of the name *Peto*. Although this was the only Peto signature we were able to decipher by Osborn's method, it was still an exciting discovery which provided another answer to the puzzle of the forged Harnett signatures.

In a parallel examination using x-ray and infrared techniques, Sheldon Keck, conservator of the Brooklyn Museum, discovered at least a half dozen other examples of painted-out Peto names on alleged Harnett paintings and continued to search for them in other soft style paintings located in museums and private collections around the country.

The identity of the person or persons who painted out the Peto names and forged Harnett's may never be known. At one point, Frankenstein was convinced that the culprit was an art dealer who had vigorously promoted Harnett paintings since 1935 and whose inventory actually included several of the soft style fakes. But this allegation proved unfounded—the art dealer apparently being fooled like many of the others. What is obvious is that the forgeries took place long after the deaths of Peto and Harnett, perhaps perpetrated by more than one person. The fact that Peto was a relatively unrecognized and prolific artist provided the opportunity for the forger to cheaply acquire large numbers of his canvasses for conversion into the much more valuable paintings of William Harnett.

The museum purchasers of the fake Harnett paintings read like a Who's Who of American art museums. Included were the Metropolitan Museum of Art, New York; the Museum of Fine Arts, Boston; the Detroit Institute of Arts; the Phillips Memorial Gallery, Washington, D. C.; the Smith College Museum of Art, North Hampton, Massachusetts; and others. As can be imagined, the results of Frankenstein's investigations were devastating to them and to the art experts who had provided attribution to the fake Harnett paintings.

But all was not lost. Exhibits featuring still life paintings of Peto's, including, paradoxically, some of the Harnett forgeries, began to appear in various museums and galleries throughout the country. Whether this was due to a resurgence of interest in Peto's paintings or to the self-serving nature of the art market is left to the reader's imagination. Whatever the cause, Peto's paintings today are almost as valuable as Harnett's.

An innocent victim of forgeries perpetrated after his death, William Harnett became an unwitting accomplice to even more massive attempts to forge his artwork during his lifetime. I developed a personal interest in this evolving story through a fortuitous acquisition of my own, but again I must depend upon Frankenstein's book *After the Hunt* to supply the details.

It all started in 1886 when Harnett painted "The Old Violin," a still life generally considered to be his most famous artwork. Following the painting's spectacular exhibit at the 1886 Cincinnati Industrial Exposition and for reasons best known to himself, Harnett sold the original oil painting and all reproduction rights to a Cincinnati lithographer by the name of Tuchfarber. He, in turn, produced literally thousands of chromolithographs (color lithographs), some on glass using a new technique he had perfected, but the largest number on paper. Tuckfarber's name, copyright line, and the date 1887 appeared in the lower right corner of the "chromos," as they became known, although a few other copies bore the inscription "ENTERED ACCORDING TO ACT OF CONGRESS IN THE YEAR 1887 BY THE DONALDSON ART SIGN CO., PUBLISHERS, COV. KY." Otherwise there is no difference between the two versions.

Tuckfarber widely advertised the chromos in Ohio newspapers, and they proved to be a hot item, selling for $15 to taverns, music stores, barber shops, libraries, offices, homes, and, in one case, a junk shop. Ed Dwight, former director of the old Milwaukee Art Institute, obtained a beautiful Donaldson Art Sign version of the chromo for me, which is now hanging in my study. The colors are absolutely magnificent despite the passage of more than a century. Under the microscope, the details are crisp and clear, and if it were not for the absence of brush strokes, I could almost imagine that it is "The Old Violin" itself—except for several curious discrepancies pointed out by Alfred Frankenstein in *After the Hunt*. Comparing the musical notes and symbols painted on the Harnett original with those on the chromo, he found several of the latter to be misplaced or omitted. Unlike Harnett, who was a skilled musician, Gus Ilg, who did the actual lithograph for Tuckfarber, knew little about music and obviously didn't attach much importance to the fundamentals of musical composition. In other respects, the chromos are amazingly faithful reproductions of the original Harnett painting.

Equally amazing are the forgeries of these chromos—hundreds of them—hanging in art galleries, museums, offices, and homes around the country, most represented to be Harnett originals. Some are close copies of the chromo, including Harnett's name on the envelope; others are adaptations from it. To believe that all of them are genuine is to believe that Harnett spent most of his life painting copies of "The Old Violin." Thanks to Gus Ilg's misplaced musical notes, many of the fakes are unmasked merely by close comparison with the Harnett original. Others fail because of inferior painting quality, dating anachronisms, or just plain stupidity on the part of the perpetrator. Among the latter are chromos passed off as original oils by cutting off the Tuckfarber identification at the bottom and elaborately reframing the copy. Others misread the Paris postmark "27 Avril 86" on the envelope, using a date in several instances after Harnett's death. Some of the paintings represent obvious put-ons. One little-known artist, Powry, replaced the envelope with the picture of a jackass inscribed on its face, "Wishing you happy days." Another substituted a picture of Charles Dickens for the envelope.

As far as I was concerned, Frankenstein's most fascinating reference was to a forgery of "The Old Violin" by none other than *John Frederick Peto*. Frankenstein does not go into great detail except to say, "Peto's version is pleasant but is not one of the artist's major achievements." What an interesting twist that an artist whose own work was used as the centerpiece of Harnett forgeries would himself be culpable of copying the great artist's work. The art world is indeed full of surprises!

But this was not my only surprise as I approached the end of a year of working in New York for A. D. Osborn. At a time when I was just beginning to get used to the confusion of the Big Apple and gaining new confidence in my own abilities as a questioned document examiner, I received a telephone call from Chicago. It was H. J. Walter, and he needed my help badly. His former associate, Alan Richardson, had decided that teaching in Canada was more suited to his temperament than examining questioned documents, and Walter was deluged with cases he could not handle alone. He had received good reports from Sellers and Osborn and knew I could do an equally good job for him. Then Walter said something I will never forget: "You know, Don, inviting you to associate with me is as much Mrs. Walter's idea as my own. We both share warm feelings for you and want to do whatever we can to advance your career."

When I told A. D. Osborn of Walter's proposal, he seemed both sad and relieved. He was about to take his own son Paul into his office, and training two assistants was more than he had bargained for. As far as I was concerned, associating with a man who had become like a father to me was a dream come true.

Friend, Teacher, Sherlock Holmes
of Handwriting Experts:
H. J. Walter's Famous Cases
Were Legion

Suitcase in hand, I stepped onto the platform at Union Station in Chicago to be greeted, not only by H. J., but by the motherly Mrs. Walter. It was obvious that she was there to see that I was properly cared for and made to feel welcome. After warm handshakes from H. J. and hugs from Mrs. Walter, I was informed that I was to stay in Wheaton with them until a room reserved at the Lawson YMCA was ready for occupancy. So, off we went to the Aurora and Elgin train station to board one of the rickety 1930 vintage electric trains that were H. J.'s principal method of transportation. That hour-long bumpy ride to Wheaton was one of many I was destined to take in the future.

At first sight, the Walter home looked like it might have been transplanted from County Surrey, England. A rose trellis framed the front door, and planters of budding, multi-colored flowers abounded everywhere. Inside the little shuttered house the décor was blue and white with English bric-a-brac placed in niches and crannies everywhere.

We had scarcely had time to settle in our chairs before Mrs. Walter scurried off into the kitchen to prepare tea. "You must get in the habit of taking a tea in the afternoon, dearie," she said. "It is very satisfying and helps you think more clearly." She was right about that. The crumbly, homemade biscuits and small sandwiches served with tea a short time later certainly satisfied the stomach of a weary traveler who hadn't been fed since leaving New York and made him think a lot about how lucky he was to have friends like this.

When I glanced out the kitchen window, I could see sparrows and finches fussing and fluttering around three or four well-stocked bird feeders. This sight served to explain an unusual ritual I later observed during noontime lunch at the office. Following his customary blood sausage sandwich, H. J. would carefully collect all of the breadcrumbs that had fallen on his newspaper tablecloth, place them in a small paper bag, and take them home for his precious birds. All in all, that charming little home and its unassuming occupants conveyed a feeling of warmth and hospitality that I will never forget.

The next morning on the train ride back to Walter's Chicago

office at 100 N. LaSalle Street, I bombarded him with questions about some of his most famous cases including the Hauptmann-Lindbergh kidnaping and the Leopold-Loeb "thrill killing" of little Bobby Franks. Following each question, Walter would say, "Oh, there wasn't really much to my testimony in that case," and quickly change the subject to my future and the training in his office. It wasn't until I mentioned the Al Capone case and a serial murder in 1946 that had Chicagoans bolting their doors that his eyes lit up.

Al Capone:
The Handwriting Finally Did Him In

"Oh, yes," he said, "I am rather proud of my part in those cases. They couldn't put Al Capone away on a murder charge, but his handwriting finally did the job." Walter went on to describe the frustration experienced by federal and local law enforcement officials who had compiled massive amounts of evidence implicating Capone in countless murder and extortion plots, only to find frightened witnesses refusing to testify at the trial or being spirited away to other parts of the country. Trying to salvage something from their investigations, prosecutors eventually charged Capone with income tax evasion, a charge for which he was finally convicted. Capone spent the remainder of his years in a federal penitentiary.

At the trial, Walter was one of the key witnesses for the prosecution, testifying that Al Capone did, in fact, endorse his name to a check made payable to the Laramie Kennel Club of Chicago, one of his many fictitious enterprises. The handwriting part of this case was comparatively simple, Walter told me. Capone made very little attempt to disguise his signature, and the comparison exhibits he prepared convincingly showed that Capone had lied about not endorsing the check. After Capone's conviction, however, someone passed around the rumor that all of the witnesses who testified against Capone were going to be murdered. So the States Attorney assigned to Walter, a big, burly guard, who stayed in his office during the day and went home with him at night. "The blighter tried to get me to carry a gun, too," said Walter, "but I figured no self-respecting Englishman would arm himself even in self-defense." It was Mrs. Walter who finally settled the matter by telling the States Attorney, "That guard is doing no good—he's just making us nervous. Anyway, who would want to shoot my Herbie? He's never hurt anybody in his life."

During the six-month period that I worked in Herbert J. Walter's office, I learned more about handwriting than in all of my years before or since. In Canada, Walter had not only examined documents for authenticity, but also taught penmanship in the public schools and became highly skilled in the art of calligraphy. This background gave him insights into handwriting identification and suspected forgery cases that few in the field

Known Signatures

) keys to said box, which I agree to return upon :

Questioned Signature

For DEPOSIT
THE LARAMIE KEN

Capone used the nickname "Al" for signing his name to the questioned check at the bottom. In other respects the signature agreed closely with the known specimens above. Note the heavy pressure exerted on the pen at the finish of the *C*, the long beginning to the *a*, and the open *o*.

could equal. The opportunity to learn from such a talented individual would serve me well in the future.

Walter saved every handwritten and typewritten envelope that came into the office. He would plop the handwritten ones down in front of me and ask, "What system of writing did this person learn?" If the writing came from overseas, which was frequently the case, he would block off the postmark and say, "Tell me about the foreign system this person was taught." I first learned about the Spencerian writing system from Walter, the recognition of which was vital to my later examination of the Texas Tatum will. Walter was not living at the time that case was tried, but if he had been, I am sure I would have called him on the phone to say thank you for the diligent training he gave me on the subject of handwriting systems. He, in turn, would probably have asked me for a detailed explanation of my trial testimony and of anything I might have done wrong to bring about the unfortunate jury verdict.

Placing the address on a typewritten envelope in front of me, Walter would say, "Tell me, Don, what kind of typewriter produced this address." If the answer was not immediately forthcoming, I could count on being mildly rebuked and given an illustrated handbook to study, dealing with comparisons of type fonts from different manufacturers of typewriters. Then he would say, "What are the unique and identifying features of this particular typewriting? What would you say about it if you were in court?" This training I received from H. J. Walter stood me in good stead during the course of the Alger Hiss case, when the history of Woodstock typewriter N230,099 came into dispute.

I testified several times in Cook County courts during this period and could always count on being asked for a replay on what took place after I got back to the office. "Did the attorney follow your suggested qualifying and direct examination questions? Did you cover all of the points set forth in your outline of proposed testimony? Did you remember to look at the jury when testifying? Did you make sure that they could all see your comparison exhibits? What questions were asked on cross-examination, and what were your responses?"

One aspect of the law I found difficult to understand in those early days when I was beginning to testify in court on a regular basis was the reliance placed by judges on past appellate court decisions, some of which were extremely critical of testimony by questioned document experts. These appellate court opinions, known as "legal precedents," are printed as the final word, not of God, but of judges anointed with a title that makes them experts in everything. Junior members of law firms spend countless hours in law libraries looking for citations that might bolster the position of their client in the eyes of the court or tear down that of their opponents. This system may work well enough where questions of admissibility of evidence and prevailing law are concerned but frequently fails miserably in the arena of scientific evidence. The trial court or "fact finding" part of the legal system may be poorly informed or completely ignorant of the subject under discussion and, what is worse, might be downright antagonistic to the expert testifying about it. In jury trials, the Court's attitude may have an equally detrimental effect upon the weight the jury gives to expert testimony. When this prejudice is then passed along to appellate court justices, disaster may result.

Illinois has had a particularly dismal record of ill-conceived appellate court decisions running back to the 1930s—with one bad opinion seemingly feeding on earlier decisions that were even worse. For example, one Illinois appellate judge wrote: "The testimony of a handwriting expert is at best secondary evidence and merely an opinion as opposed to a positive fact, and however expert the witness may be, he is not giving voice to any direct statement of fact capable of proof but only to an opinion."

At the same time, more progressive appellate courts such as one in Nebraska were finding: "Testimony of handwriting experts that the signature on an instrument offered for probate as a will is not the signature of the alleged testator, if based on sound reasons and circumstances supporting that theory, may be sufficient to overturn the testimony of subscribing witnesses that they saw the will signed. There is no presumption either in favor of witnesses or in favor of circumstances."

The Illinois decisions, oddly enough, ran counter to the views of one of the country's most vigorous and respected educators and legal scholars, John Henry Wigmore, Dean of Chicago's Northwestern University Law School. Through his writings and lectures, Wigmore and his disciples urged lawyers and judges to learn more about scientific evidence, to read the books and to employ competent experts to aid them in civil and criminal trials.

Both Wigmore and Fred Inbau, his scientific evidence successor at Northwestern University, cried out against appellate court decisions based upon archaic ideas of expert testimony and said they could only lead to miscarriages of justice. How prophetic Wigmore and Inbau were!

In the summer of 1948, I helped Herbert J. Walter prepare trial exhibits for a Chicago will contest, Jones vs. Jones, involving the purported signature of Lucy E. Jones on her last will and testament. In my wildest dreams I would not have imagined that this case, which involved overwhelming evidence of forgery, would add more fuel to the already raging fire of adverse Illinois Appellate Court decisions. But it did, and it involved that most expert of all handwriting experts, H. J. Walter, and his new assistant, Donald Doud.

Jones vs. Jones:
Illinois Appellate Court Bunglers at Work

To quote me the authority of precedents leaves me quite unmoved. All human progress has been made by ignoring precedents. If mankind had continued to be the slave of precedent we should still be living in caves and subsisting on shellfish and wild berries.

VISCOUNT PHILIP SNOWDON, 1933

Lucy E. Jones had three children—two daughters, Florence and Alice, and a son Harold. When Lucy died at the age of eighty-four, a will was produced by the two daughters leaving everything to them and nothing to Harold. Attorneys for Harold Jones promptly brought suit to overthrow the will on the grounds of forgery.

Herbert J. Walter was employed by the contestant to the will and pronounced the Lucy Eloise Jones signature on the will to be a crude forgery. The lawyers for daughters Alice and Florence employed no experts to refute the allegations, relying only upon the alleged witnessing of the will by two friends of their mother.

I can remember thinking, as I prepared the principal trial exhibits for Walter's use in court: Boy, H. J. should have an easy time proving this one—what a terrible forgery!

In the trial of the case before Circuit Judge C. J. Harrington, Walter testified that the Lucy Eloise Jones signature on the will was a traced forgery—traced from a genuine signature containing her middle name "Eloise" rather than the usual initial "E." While the model signature used for the tracing could not be located (nor could any other examples of the full name Lucy Eloise Jones), the presence of erased and unerased pencil running adjacent to the strokes of the name were proof positive of the tracing method employed. In addition, the signature itself had a clumsy, drawn appearance with several joined and mended strokes adding to the evidence of forgery. Lucy E. Jones's own signature dated during this same period of time was written freely, naturally, and continuously.

Walter then attempted to explain to Judge Harrington how the tracing of the Lucy Eloise Jones signature was accomplished. The

COMPARISON CHART

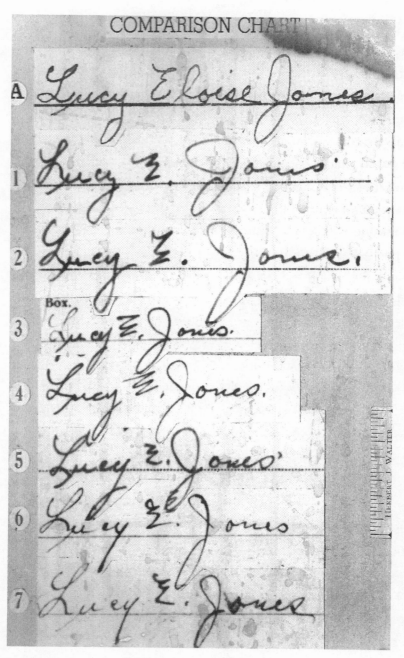

Comparison chart of Lucy E. Jones signatures.

first requirement, he said, was a transmitted light source such as a light box that would serve to illuminate the genuine signature sandwiched beneath the questioned will. Then, using a graphite pencil, the faint outline of the underlying signature was traced onto the upper document, and that image in turn traced over in pen and ink. As might be expected, the dual tracing effort produced a poor replication of Jones's signature. Moreover, unerased pencil lines were still visible in certain areas bordering the ink.

Countering Walter's testimony, the two sisters claimed that their mother suffered a mild heart attack a month of so before the signing of the will and, in addition, she had lost her glasses and could not see without them. That was why the writing was so shaky and unnatural looking. The two witnesses to the will testified in the vaguest of terms about the alleged signing.

In closing argument, the attorney for the contestant, Harold Jones, pointed out how ridiculous the sisters' contentions were. If the heart attack had affected her ability to write and the missing glasses her ability to see, how was it that there were so many carefully joined strokes throughout the signature and it was placed so methodically on the signature line? Moreover, the known signatures of Lucy Eloise Jones, signed within weeks of the questioned signature, showed no evidence whatsoever of writing difficulty. And what about the pencil evidence of tracing?

When Walter came back to the office after testifying in the case, I can remember him commenting, "Well, Don, we sure overwhelmed them with evidence. I don't see how Judge

Harrington could possibly find this will signature to be genuine."
But the two of us could not have been more wrong, for Judge
Harrington in his decision at the conclusion of the case stated:
"This Court finds the will of Lucy Eloise Jones to be genuinely
signed by Testator. The testimony of two eye witnesses to the
signing of the will cannot be overcome by any amount of expert
testimony."

Months later when Judge Harrington's decision was appealed
to the Illinois Supreme Court, Justice Gunn, in his summation
upholding the lower Court ruling, drafted an even more venomous
opinion that has shackled questioned document experts in Illinois
to this day. He wrote, in part: "Expert testimony has its useful
place, but being an opinion, it has less weight than direct
testimony on a controverted fact. It is not the policy of the law to
permit acts positively established by eyewitnesses to be overcome
by opinions, except possibly when the eyewitnesses have been
discredited or impeached. To do so would put a premium upon
secondary evidence, [a term obviously adopted from earlier
decisions] not justified by any known rule of law."

In Transition

In the latter part of 1948 it became apparent that I would need
surgery to correct a condition brought on by my pneumothorax
treatment for tuberculosis. So, in January of 1949, I bade a sad

farewell to the Walters and returned to Los Angeles where I became one of the first patients to undergo a "decortication" operation designed to reexpand my right lung. Fortunately, the procedure proved to be successful, and after six months of recuperation, I was champing at the bit to get back into the questioned document field. And, again, it was my good friend Herbert J. Walter who showed me the way.

In one of a series of letters written to me while I was recuperating, Walter suggested that, since he had been forced to hire a new assistant to fill my former job in his office, he would be willing to contact John F. Tyrrell of Milwaukee to see if he would be interested in employing me as his associate. I had visited Tyrrell on several occasions during my stay with Walter, primarily to assist him with cases requiring microscopic studies or technical photography. Tyrrell at that time was eighty-nine years of age and suffered from a severe case of glaucoma. "I may be partially blind," he would say, "but I can still see twice as good with what's left as those damnable graphologists" (referring to individuals who professed the ability to tell character and personality from handwriting and also set themselves out to be forensic handwriting experts). But despite his physical problems, this indomitable, ingratiating little man still accepted cases and managed somehow to hobble to the courthouse when testimony was required. Circulatory problems had forced the removal of most of his toes. I never had the privilege of seeing Tyrrell testify in court, but I was told his customary attire was a cutaway coat, grey striped pants, and spats to match. What a spectacle he must have been to the judge or jury!

I always looked forward to these visits with John Tyrrell, for he was a true pioneer in the questioned document field. Once his reminiscences about past cases were out of the way, we had many a spirited conversation about difficult document problems, some of which he had resolved with most ingenious solutions. Tyrrell was a true innovator in the field and was highly respected by fellow questioned document examiners.

Despite our common interests and the technical help I was able to give him, Tyrrell never indicated in any way that he would ever want me or anyone else to associate with him. I am convinced that this indomitable little man thought he could continue examining documents until he was 100 years of age.

So it was with considerable surprise that shortly after my last communication with Walter I received an interesting telephone call from Milwaukee. "This is John Tyrrell," said a voice that I immediately recognized—although did I detect a quavering note to that cultured speech? "Mr. Doud," continued Tyrrell, "do you remember me? We met several years ago at a convention of the American Society of Questioned Document Examiners." Oops, I thought to myself, doesn't he remember that within the last year I helped him with several cases in Milwaukee? "The reason I am calling," he continued, "is to invite you to come to Milwaukee to eventually take over my practice. You know, I am eighty-nine years of age and," with a chuckle, "I guess it's about time I retired. H. J. Walter tells me you have fully recovered from lung surgery and might be interested in a proposition of this kind. You would not only be taking over a lucrative practice but a name that I would modestly claim is known worldwide. What do you say?"

I nearly dropped the phone from excitement as I stammered, "Sounds like a great idea to me, Mr. Tyrrell. When do you want me to come out?" Thus began an association of three years duration, primarily notable for its education of one young man in the unpredictability and obstinacy of a talented, proud old man who had not quite come to terms with his own mortality.

So, again I packed up my suitcase, this time for what I hoped would be a final move to Milwaukee, Wisconsin.

13

Following in the Footsteps of a Feisty Octogenarian Raconteur

John Tyrrell's Cases Ran Back to the Turn of the Twentieth Century

John Tyrrell's office in the Wisconsin Building hadn't changed much since my earlier visits. Seated behind his huge oak desk set diagonally in one corner of the room, the eighty-nine-year-old icon with his shock of white hair, watery eyes, and formal attire right down to his bow tie, tottered to his feet as I approached and greeted me with a friendly wave of the hand. "Good to see you, Don. I have a lot of things to tell you." Before he could get started on what I suspected would be reminiscences of his famous cases of the past, I broke in to inquire about more mundane things such as where I was going to eat and sleep that night. "Oh, yes," he said, "I believe Anna (Anna Carpenter, his daughter) has gotten you a room at the YMCA, and there is a restaurant right next door." Well, at least this was a beginning. Now I could listen to his stories secure in my knowledge that, after he was through, my creature comforts would be taken care of.

John Tyrrell was a friend and contemporary of Albert S. Osborn and participated with him in many of the famous document cases of the early years. His memory for every detail of these cases was phenomenal, and as an accomplished raconteur, he would spend hours talking about them. And who could blame him? The list read like a who's who of famous criminal trials including the Mollineaux society poisoning, tried in 1898; the Hauptmann-Lindbergh kidnaping; State of Illinois vs. Heirens; State of Illinois vs. Leopold and Loeb, Allis-Chalmers CIO stuffed ballot case, all tried during the early part of the twentieth century.

From the perspective of my own career, the case of Tyrrell's that stood out from all the rest was the New York Rice-Patrick murder trial that took place in 1902.

Rice-Patrick Case:
Tragedy Strikes a Hughes Ancestor

William Marsh Rice was a wealthy, eighty-five-year-old Texan who, during an earlier period of his life, founded the Rice Institute for the Advancement of Literature Science and Art, now known as Rice University. After the death of his wife in 1896,

Following in the Footsteps
of a Feisty Octogenarian Raconteur

Rice migrated to New York to live, as he put it, "the good life," taking with him a trusted valet and secretary, Charles F. Jones. As it happened, the dream of the "good life" turned into a nightmare when Albert T. Patrick, an itinerant lawyer, conspired with the "trusted" valet to kill the old man, first by attempting to poison him with cyanide, and finally by application of chloroform.

When interrogated by the police as to the circumstances surrounding Rice's death, Jones, to their astonishment, almost immediately broke down and admitted that, at Patrick's behest, he had killed the old man while he was in bed. Jones then described how he clapped a chloroform-soaked rag over Rice's mouth while he was asleep and, as the old man struggled into wakefulness, had held him to the bed with his own body until breathing ended. Jones subsequently turned state's evidence while placing all the blame on Patrick for instigating the plot. Because of some quirk in the law, Jones never served a day in prison for his crime.

At Patrick's trial for plotting the murder of Rice and for forging a number of Rice's signatures, John Tyrrell testified that the W. M. Rice signatures appearing on the four pages of a will leaving virtually all of Rice's multi-million-dollar estate to Patrick were traced forgeries. Tracing, Tyrrell explained to the jury, was a method of forgery requiring use of a transmitted light source such as a light box to illuminate a genuine signature sandwiched beneath the document to be forged. The outline of the underlying signature is then followed as accurately as possible by the forger. When the same tracing model is used for a number of forged signatures, all of them tend to look alike in size, proportion, spacing, and letter formation—absent the natural variation inherent in genuine signatures.

Tyrrell demonstrated his opinion by photographing the four will signatures under transparent plates with ruled grids, the lines of which intersected various portions of the signatures in almost precisely the same places. The known signatures of Rice varied substantially one from the others, as was to be expected.

Then, using a crayon and large pad of paper, Tyrrell demonstrated, to the fascination of the jury, differences in the shading of the ink strokes produced by the dual-nib flexible point pens. (Pens of this kind are seldom seen today. Ball pens now dominate the writing instrument market.) "In his genuine signatures," said Tyrrell, "Rice held the pen with its far end pointing towards his body. This position of the pen produced shading *on the downstrokes*. The forger of the will signatures rotated his hand and pen towards the right, thereby producing shading *on the horizontal strokes*. "And why did he hold the pen in this fashion?" continued Tyrrell. "It was to better follow the dim outline of the underlying signature without blocking the view with his writing hand.

As Tyrrell spoke, each point was driven home by skillfully drawn examples of hands holding pens in various positions. One newspaper published the day following Tyrrell's testimony referred to him as "The Wizard of the Pen." Another said of his testimony, "It was a kind of an x-ray upon handwriting."

At the conclusion of the lengthy trial, the jury convicted Albert

Patrick of first degree murder and sentenced him to life imprisonment. Several years later a politically motivated governor pardoned Patrick completely.

Charred Documents: He Turned Black Into White

Despite his involvement in many nationally known cases, Tyrrell was probably the most proud of his work in an obscure little case having its origin in Chetek, Wisconsin. I have heard Tyrrell's story about the case on more occasions than I care to mention, but I continued to be impressed with the ingenious way he went about solving it.

Tyrrell, like many of the other early pioneers, was first and foremost a problem solver, and if it cost him weeks of experimentation with little or no compensation, so be it. The thought of defeat was never in Tyrrell's mind, and this new case represented one of his toughest challenges.

The year was 1924. A four-alarm fire had completely demolished the home of an elderly couple, killing them and burning all of their possessions including a strongbox full of irreplaceable records. What was in the box? Nobody knew, but it was important to find out. When the warped strongbox full of charred documents was delivered to Tyrrell's office, "I could see,"

Tyrrell said, "that this was going to be the most challenging and time-consuming job I had ever undertaken. There was very little guidance available in the literature, and I would have to do my own pioneering work." And pioneer he did. After several weeks of frustrating research with chemicals, infrared and ultraviolet photography, Tyrrell finally recalled reading in some arson-related journal that charred fragments continued to emit gasses for a period of time following the initial burning. If those emissions somehow or other corresponded to the materials originally on the documents, such as printing or handwriting, perhaps there was some way of recording the information. Tyrrell's explanation follows:

> My first thought was of photographic negatives, but these materials are sensitive to the light coming through a camera lens, and as far as I knew, nobody had ever used them to record gasses. But there was no harm in trying, so I took several of the charred fragments into the darkroom, turned off the light, and placed them between two unexposed photographic plates. I then wrapped the plates in several layers of black, light-tight paper, packed them in boxes for additional protection, and went on a three-weeks vacation.
>
> When I got home from our trip and went into the darkroom to develop the negatives, I was fully expecting to see nothing—nothing but a perfectly

transparent plate. Instead, to my delight, I found images of printing and handwriting that were as sharp and clear as any taken through the lens of my camera. The prints I made from these negatives helped the executors evaluate the holdings of the man and wife who died in the file.

Tyrrell often bragged that his three weeks exposure on photographic film was the world record holder, but he didn't live long enough to see it beat by months or years when astro-photography of the planets and stars came into common use.

Two years after our tumultuous association in the Alger Hiss case, John Tyrrell's eyesight and circulatory problems became so bad that he was forced to enter a nursing facility. On one of my visits, this indomitable little man introduced me to the fundamentals of Braille, which he was learning from a fellow resident. On every occasion, I could expect to hear repeated, in exquisite detail, stories of his most famous cases. The Alger Hiss case in which he participated largely as my observer was not included. I think he always felt somewhat embarrassed by our involvement with that case, even though my findings were adverse to Hiss's contentions.

14

Reflections on a Life and a Profession

I am sitting here in my study surrounded by case files and notes, awash in memories of the past. It has been almost a decade since I started writing this book, and now that it is almost finished, I am already feeling a sense of loss–as though the writing of each chapter has taken a chunk out of my life, and given it away to succeeding generations. But it is a loss I will gladly bear if I have been able to convey to the reader a sense of what it was like to be an early worker in my field, to participate in some of the notable, and not so notable, cases of my time, and to be thrust into the company of some of the great questioned document pioneers of an earlier generation.

Fifty years have passed since I first came to Milwaukee to associate with John Tyrrell and, as the reader of this book may have gathered, I too have become a "feisty octogenarian raconteur." But this book is not just a collection of stories about my most famous cases and those of my mentors and associates; it

Don Doud, about 1990.

also deals with the credibility of the evidence we offered in court and how that evidence was perceived by the judges, juries, appellate courts, and the general public.

REFLECTIONS ON A LIFE AND A PROFESSION

A significant number of the cases I describe involved conflicts between experts or between expert and the trial or appellate courts. It is here that I have taken a sizeable risk to my own reputation and to that of others with whom I was associated. I have asked you, the reader, to be the final arbiter in my court of last resort. To provide a proper basis for your verdict, I have taken you into the laboratory to review the evidence and into the courtroom where our findings were put to the test. It is in this arena, where demonstrative evidence takes expert testimony out of the realm of mere opinion and into that of visible proof, that I have felt most confident in your verdict. In that connection, it is interesting to note that among the many books proclaiming the innocence of Bruno Hauptmann, Alger Hiss, and Albert Patrick, not one contains an example of the comparison exhibits prepared by the questioned document experts. Had they done so, the readers would have laughed their way through the remainder of the transparent attempts to revise history.

In the preface to this book I asked you, the reader, to take a seat in the jury box, listen to the testimony, *carefully study the exhibits*, then make your decision.

Made in the USA
Charleston, SC
28 March 2011